TWENTY ONE POSITIONS:

A Cartographic Dream of the Middle East

*Abdelfattah Abusrour,
Lisa Schlesinger &
Naomi Wallace*

BROADWAY PLAY PUBLISHING INC
224 E 62nd St, NY, NY 10065
www.broadwayplaypub.com
info@broadwayplaypub.com

Cover art by Bruce McLeod

First printing: June 2015. This printing: June 2016
I S B N: 978-0-88145-629-5

Book design: Marie Donovan
Page make-up: Adobe Indesign
Typeface: Palatino
Printed and bound in the U S A

INTRODUCTION
Robin D G Kelley

*The tradition of the oppressed teaches us that the state of
emergency in which we live is not the exception but the rule.*
—Walter Benjamin, *Theses on the Philosophy of History*

I've only been here a few days and already I can't breathe.
—Fawaz to Colonel Danny Tirza, TWENTY-ONE
POSITIONS

The genesis of this play was itself a bold cartographic
dream, a remapping of the theater world by building
bridges between the U S and Palestine. In 2002, Naomi
Wallace led a delegation of American playwrights
comprised of Robert O'Hara, Betty Shamieh, Tony
Kushner, Kia Corthron, and Lisa Schlesinger to meet
their Palestinian counterparts in the West Bank.
They connected with the theater community there to
exchange ideas and learn about the conditions under
which Palestinians worked, lived, and created. They
met Abdelfattah Abusrour, poet, playwright, educator,
and founding director of the Alrowwad Cultural and
Theatre Society located in Bethlehem's Aida Refugee
Camp. Having grown up in the camp, Abusrour gave
up a promising career in science to create a "beautiful
theater of resistance" aimed at releasing the creative
capacity of young people.

Wallace conceived of the trip not as a fact-finding mission or a liberal quest for "dialogue" but as an obligation to resist injustice and a radical act of reciprocity. Collaboration was an objective. So when she received a commission from the Guthrie Theater in Minneapolis in 2003 to create new work, she promptly recruited Abusrour and Lisa Schlesinger to co-author a play about the situation in Palestine.

It took a little over a year and two more trips to Palestine for the trio to complete "Twenty-One Positions: A Cartographic Dream of the Middle East." They wrote it during the height of the Second Intifada and as Israel began constructing its infamous 422-mile-long, twenty to twenty-six foot high "security barrier." Referred to as the "apartheid wall" by Palestinians, this gargantuan concrete structure snakes through the West Bank, razing villages and appropriating land for Israel, limiting Palestinian mobility and access to schools, farms, loved ones, and much needed medical care. Armed with electrified barbed wire, heavily policed gates and checkpoints, vehicle barrier trenches and a sixty-meter-wide "exclusion zone" on the Palestinian side, the wall was designed by Colonel Danny Tirza to be impenetrable. In 2004, the International Court of Justice ruled that the wall was illegal and ordered construction stopped. Israel has yet to abide by the ruling.

Israeli officials claim the wall was a response to the Second Intifada—the Palestinian uprising against the illegal occupation, escalating state violence, and Israel's continued violation of international law and human rights. (The First Intifada erupted in 1987 and ended in the early 1990s). The catalyst for renewed resistance was Prime Minister Ariel Sharon's visit to the Haram al-Sharif (Temple Mount), the location of the Al Aqsa Mosque, in Jerusalem's Old City on September 28,

2000. Surrounded by over 1,000 riot police, Sharon announced, "The Temple Mount is in our hands," which Muslims understood as a threat to take Al Aqsa, the world's third holiest Islamic site. Violence erupted. Palestinian resistance was met with brutal force, as the Israeli Occupation Forces launched a series of military operations and administrative policies designed to collectively punish all Palestinians.

And yet, despite what critics and pundits say about "Twenty-One Positions," it is not about the wall. Rather, the wall is both character and prop in a larger drama about six decades of colonialism. It is spectacle and obstacle, background and foreground, metaphor and smokescreen. To treat it as the play's subject is to confuse flower bulbs and olive trees for the land itself.

Abusrour, Schlesinger, and Wallace have written a brilliant, unsettling, searing, tragicomedy about the meaning and consequences of violent dispossession and military occupation on generations of human beings—consequences that extend well beyond the Green Line, from the Jordan River to the Ohio River, from the Potomac to the Tigris and Euphrates to the bloodstained beaches of Gaza. They remind us that Operations Defensive Shield, Determined Path, Autumn Clouds, Summer Rains, Cast Lead, Returning Echo, Protective Edge, Brothers' Keeper, or whatever the euphemism du jour, are not exceptional episodes but the rule. The consequences for the ruled ought not be measured merely by the destructive force of American-made F-15s, cluster bombs and white phosphorous, but also by the everyday routine of occupation—unemployment, poverty, segregated roads, insecurity, illegal settlements, state-sanctioned theft of water and land, destruction of olive trees and local agriculture, a racially defined security regime, the effects of permanent refugee existence.

Despite the walls, settlements, checkpoints, barriers, borders, envoys, articles, resolutions, and maps, there has been but one state since 1948: the state of emergency, the state of war. The play is set mainly in Bethlehem in the West Bank, but the state of emergency extends to every part of Palestine. The play's invocation of shredded maps and contested archaeological sites are powerful symbols for how the occupation and the wall break up contiguous territories and lands, disrupting lives, bludgeoning memories, rupturing history. But in Israel's efforts to create normalcy out of rupture, the rupture returns like Banquo's ghost. Palestinians are that rupture, the living, the dead, the disappeared, the imprisoned, the refugee whose presence disrupts the Zionist dream. Like eleven-year-old Rund, they walk around with broken pieces of maps and memory of how the parts fit, how to move through occupation in "seconds or minutes" in a militarized land that can take hours to move a few kilometers. Cartographic dream meets demographic nightmare.

But wait. What we have here is a love story involving two brothers, both of whom were born and raised in Cincinnati, and their exiled parents, a beautiful and brilliant bride-to-be and her equally brilliant auntie, a sagacious and hungry little girl, a dispossessed old Mizrahi Jew, an architect of war, a people and a land. To grasp this love story, one must be prepared to hold two or more contradictory ideas and dreams at once. Israeli soldiers know how to kill from twenty-one positions. Palestinian women demonstrate twenty-one positions of lovemaking. An "Operation" is generally an act of war, but an "operation" can be an act of love. Intifada and love are deeply intertwined. So is colonialism and dehumanization. Colonial war turns Israeli kids into cogs in the Occupation machine. Every interrogation, every seizure, every shooting, every strip search, every home demolition and bulldozed olive tree, dehumanizes both occupied and occupier.

For the parents of Fawaz and Rashid, exile was a strategy to preserve one's humanity in the face of colonial onslaught. But it didn't work. Exile could not suppress the longing for home, the memories, the feeling of fugitivity and rootlessness. Fawaz, especially, believed America was the better place, the paragon of democracy and the rule of law. Adamant not to do anything "illegal" in occupied Palestine, he believed his American citizenship protected him. It never occurred to Fawaz that his name, skin color, and heritage trumped his passport. (How a native of Cincinnati, where police killed young black men with impunity, where poor black residents complained of living under occupation, where skin color trumps American citizenship, could be so naïve is but one of many sly jokes slipped in by the playwrights.) The irony, of course, is that the occupation itself is illegal. And so are the settlements, Israel's use of American military supplies to maintain the occupation, home demolitions and forced evictions, prohibiting the right of return, not to mention the wall. Israel violates international law, Geneva Conventions, and U N resolutions with impunity with the full backing of Washington DC—the one place on Rund's shredded map that proves indigestible. Fawaz's disappointments are particularly striking now, for as I write these words the Palestinian Authority has successfully applied to join the International Criminal Court in an effort to bring charges against Israel for war crimes. Not only has the U S opposed their bid, but President Benjamin Netanyahu promised to retaliate by withholding at least $127 million in tax revenue owed to the Palestinian Authority.

"Twenty-One Positions" is a dangerous play. And Abusrour, Schlesinger, and Wallace know it. The Guthrie Theater decided not to produce the play, and in a letter to the playwrights, instead of critiquing the dramaturgy of the play, the Gurthrie's senior dramaturg dismissed the play as an "anti-Zionist... propaganda tract" and accused the authors of "justifying...terrorist acts". As of this writing, Fordham University mounted the only U S production of "Twenty-One Positions."

What makes the play dangerous is not its explicit critique of occupation or its refusal to "balance" Palestinian pain and suffering with Israeli pain and suffering. Occasionally, the theater gathers enough courage to stage these kinds of stories. "Twenty-One Positions" is dangerous because its main characters resist dehumanization; they refuse to accept the terms and conditions of colonial rule; they reject victimization. They are dangerous because they are real. They represent the activists, the intellectuals, the youth, who speak confidently about a liberated country, who see the old guard leadership and the Palestinian Authority as impediments, who envision and debate at least twenty-one different paths to a democratic and decolonized future, who keep the shredded maps and the keys and the memories. You see, I met the likes of Rashid, Hala, and Fawaz at Birzeit University, at various Palestinian think-tanks in Ramallah and Haifa, and at my own university. I drank coffee with Maryam and watched Rund take off on her battered bike along the narrow pathways of a Bethlehem refugee camp. They are the ones trying desperately to breathe, to think, to live, to fulfil their own cartographic dreams of replacing the state of emergency with one land—surveyed from a glider cutting through a clear, quiet, smokeless sky.

TWENTY ONE POSITIONS: A CARTOGRAPHIC DREAM OF THE MIDDLE EAST was commissioned by The Guthrie Theater.

The Fordham University Theatre Program (Artistic Director, Matthew Maguire) in association with The Public Theater, in 2008, first produced the play.

FAWAZ AL HAJ	Ian Quinlan
RASHID AL HAJ	Chris Larkin
RUND	Marjuan Canady
HALA	Jessica Farr
DANNY T	Ronan Babbitt
MURAD SALIH DANIEL	Jacob Wallach
MARYAM	Jillian Goins
SOLDIER #1	Chris Masullo
SOLDIER #2	Julia Zangrilli
SOLDIER #3	Tom Pecinka

Director	Lisa Peterson
Scenic designer	Rachel Hauck
Costume designer	Michelle Phillips
Lighting designer	Chad McArver
Sound designer	Lindsay Jones
Composer	Gina Leishman
Musician	Zafer Tawil
Properties designer	Teralyn Bruketta
Stage manager	Donald Fried
Production manager	Kai Brothers
Dramaturg	Mandy Hackett

CHARACTERS & SETTING

FAWAZ AL HAJ, *American, late twenties*
RASHID AL HAJ, FAWAZ's *younger brother*
HALA, *bride-to-be of* RASHID, *Palestinian*
RUND, *eleven year old girl, Palestinian*
DANNY T, *Israeli, master-builder and architect of the Wall*
MURAD SALIH DANIEL, *from Baghdad, Israeli*
MARYAM, *aunt of* HALA, *Palestinian*
CHORUS *of three Israeli soldiers*

Time: Now, and the past.

Place: Bethlehem, West Bank, as it might remember itself, in reverie. The Wall is staggering, always there, but neither obvious nor concrete.

"And so I think you should stay here with your sword drawn if you're set on it and your anger is big enough. You have good cause, I admit. But if your anger is a short one, you'd better go."
Bertolt Brecht, MOTHER COURAGE

"When was the last time we slept without dreaming we died."
Nathalie Handal, *The Lives Of Rain*

ACT ONE

Prologue

(Fawaz walks out onto a stage which is bare but for a single toy-size model hang glider that is suspended from above. He is not yet fully dressed, a jacket and tie hang over his arm, and he carries a simple, old fashioned square suitcase. He puts the suitcase down. Fawaz sets the glider gently spinning, and keeps his eye on it as he buttons up his shirt. Then he begins to put on his tie. After some moments, Rashid appears, from another time/space. He carries a simple chair. Rashid helps Fawaz with his tie: they are now teenagers again.)

RASHID: Your hands are sweating.

(Fawaz tries to wrestle his tie from Rashid but Rashid wins out.)

RASHID: Let me do it. Girls don't like sweaty hands.

FAWAZ: How would you know? You've never had a girl.

RASHID: Yeah, but at night I have them one by one and damn are they sweet.

FAWAZ: Shhh. Mom'll hear you. *(Beat)* Make sure Dad takes his meds before he goes to sleep. If he doesn't, he'll feel it in his hip all week. And make sure Mom gets

FAWAZ/RASHID: her hot milk and piece of toast.

FAWAZ: I'll be home before eleven.

RASHID: It's a drag having old parents. I can't remember them without grey hair. I'm sixteen years old and my father looks like the Pope.

FAWAZ: Don't fuck up again. Last time I went out you forgot to let the cat out so it pissed on the Persian. You fed the canary a whole peanut, not halved like I told you, and it choked.

RASHID: To death, yeah. Mom is still pissed. *(He has finished FAWAZ's tie. He gets FAWAZ's jacket ready, picks off some lint, smoothes it.)* But she's still gonna lend me the eighty bucks to get the motor on my glider rejigged!

FAWAZ: I'll rejig your ass if I come home and anything is out of place.

RASHID: You know, when you turn eighteen you're supposed to be cool. You are definitely not cool, Fawaz. And this jacket proves it. Yuck. Looks like Granddad's.

FAWAZ: Yeah? Well at least I've got a working plan. For both of us—

RASHID: *(Mocks)* —for the rest of our lives?

FAWAZ: Damn right. First we go to University—

RASHID: *(Interrupts)* Not "we", bro. I told you I've got other—

FAWAZ: *(Interrupts)* Yes, "we". Both of us together. Now shut up about it.

(RASHID helps FAWAZ into his jacket, they are silent some moments.)

RASHID: When I'm up in that glider, there's no plan and all of it's just wide open space. Up in that thing, I'm God's right hand man.

FAWAZ: Up in that thing you're an idiot as much as you are down here. Open your books for a change. You're gonna fail chemistry. I'm warning you.

RASHID: I got to tell you something. Something private.

FAWAZ: If this is about your erections I don't want to hear it.

RASHID: No. No. That time we were at the State Fair and I saw my first hang-glider?

(FAWAZ just looks at RASHID, resisting this conversation.)

RASHID: The Mosquito! Yeah. By Swedish Aerosport. Commonly known as Mozzie. Thereafter known to me as The Mozz. I didn't realize it at the time but we were looking at the new N R G model, with streamlined front entry harness,

(Now FAWAZ relents and joins the excitement with RASHID.)

FAWAZ: electric start,

RASHID: Radne-Raket

FAWAZ: One hundred C C two-stroke engine,

RASHID: with ten horsepower at eighty-eight hundred R P M.

FAWAZ: Fan cooled, clutch equipped

RASHID: with de-compressor for easy pull starts. The largest pilot to fly with that system was one-point-nine-eight meters tall and weighed

FAWAZ: A hundred and ten kilograms. Naked weight.

(RASHID taps the model glider and they both watch it turn.)

FAWAZ: That glider moved above us like an eraser 'cross the sky. *(Now he makes the buzzing sound of a motor as he watches the glider spin.)*

RASHID: And I, Rashid Al Haj, was one of those notions it wiped clean: an eleven year old Arab, an American citizen, a non-practicing Muslim at Ranger Grade School for Catholic Boys, just standing there, looking up, with one hard, surprisingly painful erection.

(FAWAZ *stops the buzzing sound.*)

FAWAZ: I knew it. It's always about your dick!

RASHID: But the Mozz wasn't only my first sexual experience: it was my first love. After a rush like that, I was enlisted as a lover-for-life of that impossible, contraptual vision:

FAWAZ/RASHID: (*Together*) The Motorized Hang glider.

(*Suddenly* FAWAZ *and* RASHID *just stare at one another. Neither moves.* FAWAZ *is now his adult self once more.*)

FAWAZ: Where the hell are you, Rashid?

RASHID: (*Shrugs*) I don't know. But I know where you are.

FAWAZ: Oh yeah?

(RASHID *spins* FAWAZ *around and sits him down in the chair.*)

RASHID: You've got no date tonight. Matter of fact, I'd guess you haven't had a date in a while.

(RASHID *slips off his belt and uses it as a seat belt across* FAWAZ*'s lap and around the chair. He pulls the "seat belt" tight. Now we begin to hear the distant sound of a motor, slowly getting louder.*)

RASHID: And you're on a 747 KLM night flight from Cincinnati through Amsterdam to Tel Aviv, bro. And you ate too many pretzels. Took you to pretzel-land.

FAWAZ: Where are you?

(RASHID *won't answer.*)

FAWAZ: I'd like to hit you, you irresponsible son of a bitch. For leaving us.

RASHID: That was years ago.

FAWAZ: Fucking feels like right now. Not a word from you in years. Nothing. Until now.

RASHID: 'Cause I'm getting married!

FAWAZ: I don't believe it.

RASHID: Neither do I! And you, my brother, are going to be my best man.

FAWAZ: No I'm not.

RASHID: Yes you are. You're already on your way. *(He disappears.)*

FAWAZ: But I will come and find you 'cause Mom told me not to come back without you. And after I kick your ass for all the damage you did by leaving us, I'm going to stuff a rag in your mouth, fold you into my fucking suitcase and ship you home!

(FAWAZ is alone again. The motor sound of the jet grows enormous, then dead silence some moments before an explosion. He is startled, and "wakes", having landed. We hear over the intercom a smooth voice: "Welcome to Ben Gurion Airport". Blackout)

(End Prologue)

Scene One

(FAWAZ, carrying his suitcase, has arrived at the airport in Tel Aviv. He holds his passport tightly against his chest. Three officials, as the CHORUS, are played by Israeli soldiers They are seated in wheeled office chairs. Two of the CHORUS are pushing the third back and forth, across the length of the stage. As though the chairs were a part of their bodies, they move with grace and rapidity. At one point the officials,

seated in their 'flying' chairs, will circle FAWAZ. FAWAZ
hardly moves in the scene, only if he must get out of the way.
What we witness here is the confidence, even grace, of a well
managed bureaucracy.)

Song of the Welcome to Ben Gurion Airport

ALL CHORUS: We can read you, we can see you, like a
  shiny pane of glass.
We can hear you, we can taste you, we can even pinch
  your ass.
We are kindly and intelligent, we are members of the
  club.
But we have got a job to do so we do it, there's no rub.
We've got enemies beyond the gate and evil that will
  creep.
We've got bang, bang in our front yards and bang,
  bang in our sleep.

CHORUS 1: What holidays do you desecrate?

FAWAZ: Bethlehem.

CHORUS 2: What language do you celebrate?

FAWAZ: I need to get to Bethlehem.

*(*CHORUS *sings various lines, sometimes together, sometimes*
apart. FAWAZ *speaks his lines)*

FAWAZ: I'm a U S citizen.

CHORUS: He's an American guy, from the sweet Ohio
  State.
Owns his little store, a good worker, never late.

FAWAZ: I have my own line of products.

CHORUS:
Has his own line of products. He knows who he be.

Got a store that sells nutrition—

FAWAZ: —and home-made Vitamin E.

CHORUS: You are what we know you are, red blooded
  through and through.
But we know your little secret and we know you know
  we do.

FAWAZ: Could you please hurry it up—

CHORUS: Be a good boy, brush your teeth. Say thank
  you if you please.
You'll have a pleasant journey if you mind your Qs
  and Ps.

FAWAZ: I need to get to my brother's wedding.

CHORUS: Oh, look at that, a down cast face, he doesn't
  like protection!
This is for you we do this dance, so please don't feel
  rejection.
But my God this is a banquet, said the termite to the
  house.
I'm going to call my embassy, said the cheese to the
  mouse.
No need to call your embassy, of course we'll let you
  pass.

But one thing 'fore you do, one small thing we have to
  ask:

ALL CHORUS:
Is he innocent? Is he innocent? Is he innocent as can be?
Fawaz al Haj. Is he an innocent to a T?

FAWAZ: Of course I'm innocent!

(Singing the following fast:)

CHORUS 1: Said the rectum to the hose.

CHORUS 2: Said the finger to the nose.

CHORUS 3: Said the dance to the pose.

CHORUS 2: Put on your clothes.

ALL CHORUS: Welcome to Israel.

(FAWAZ leaves immigration. The CHORUS signals to other visitors, and the public, to enter Israel. The CHORUS now wave tiny Israeli flags.)

ALL CHORUS: Welcome. Welcome. Welcome Home. Welcome to Israel. Welcome home.

(End Scene One)

Scene Two

(Bethlehem. RUND is wearing her school back pack. She does a backward hopscotch.)

RUND: *(Chants, first in Arabic, then in English)*
Jaras
Elmadrassah run
Wel ostath inj jun
Welkutub ibtekra lahalha
Wel aklam bitnam

I can hear the school bell.
The teacher's getting mad.
The books are reading by themselves,
The pencils acting bad.

(Suddenly FAWAZ's suitcase comes crashing across the stage. Followed by FAWAZ, who stumbles and trips, hitting the ground, having been shoved hard from behind. FAWAZ dusts himself off, enraged at this treatment. He shouts back at the checkpoint:)

FAWAZ: I'm gonna report your big ass to my embassy! You can count on that! *(To himself)* Stupid son of a bitch… *(To checkpoint)* Sissy! *(To himself)* Two damn hours to get through. *(To checkpoint)* Ass-bone…

(FAWAZ sits on his suitcase to look at his map. Then he notices RUND, standing near him, silently observing his outburst.)

RUND: I take it that was your first checkpoint? You have a dirty mouth.

FAWAZ: And you have a dirty face, kid. You know where the Saraya Hall is?

RUND: You're from the other side of the wall.

FAWAZ: Yep.

RUND: Israeli side.

FAWAZ: The Whatever Side.

RUND: That side used to be this side.

FAWAZ: The Saraya Hall. You know it or not?

RUND: Maybe I do.

FAWAZ: I'm looking for a wedding. The Al Haj wedding?

RUND: Maybe I don't.

FAWAZ: Could you show me on this map?

(RUND snatches his map.)

RUND: I know maps.

FAWAZ: Hey, give it back!

RUND: I can fix your map. *(She tears off a small piece of the map.)*

FAWAZ: I just bought that!

RUND: The Saraya Hall? Try Tulkarm first.

(RUND tears off another small piece and lets it fall to the ground. With each village or town she tears a small piece and lets it fall. As she walks and tears, FAWAZ follows behind, trying to pick up the pieces of map.)

RUND: Then try Qalqilya. Or Salfit. Or Nablus.

FAWAZ: Stop that you brat!

RUND: Then Bil'in and up to Tubas. Down again to Ramallah, across to Jericho, zip zip back to Abu Dis,

FAWAZ: You're gonna buy me a new one!

RUND: through Beit Sahour, then Bethlehem, skip skip over to Hebron. Oh Hebron. Or slip through Alquds-Jerusalem. And then the little places.

(FAWAZ *gives up.*)

FAWAZ: Damn it.

(RUND *tears even smaller pieces.*)

FAWAZ: Qalandia. Dahiet-Al-Bareed. Beit Hanina. Sho'fat. AT-Tur. Beit Safafa. Sur Bahir. Rashid Al-Haj. Um Tuba.

FAWAZ: Wait. Rashid Al-Haj?

RUND: Beit Safafa. Checkpoint number 303.

FAWAZ: That's my brother. You know my brother? He was supposed to meet me at the airport and he didn't show. The bastard. Just like him to leave me stranded.

RUND: Have you seen my cousin Hala?

FAWAZ: Hala?

RUND: She's the bride. Looks like morning even when it's night, that's what they say.

FAWAZ: Take me to her.

RUND: What will you give me?

FAWAZ: I don't know. What do you want?

RUND: One of your socks.

FAWAZ: Huh?

RUND: One of your socks or no deal.

FAWAZ: I need my socks.

RUND: So do I. Lost one of mine at a checkpoint.

FAWAZ: How'd you do that?

RUND: It didn't hold up to interrogation.

(RUND *holds out her hand.* FAWAZ *finally takes off his shoe, and his sock, and drapes it in her hand. She sniffs it.*)

RUND: This sock has travelled. Yuck.

FAWAZ: Didn't have time to change.

(RUND *puts on his sock. She now wears one long adult sock and her little one.*)

RUND: How do I look?

FAWAZ: Take me to my brother's fiancée. (*Looking down at her mismatched socks.*)

RUND: They do not match.

FAWAZ: Of course they don't. I'm twice your size.

RUND: They'll tease me on the playground. If I can find the playground…

FAWAZ: Look, kid. Get going. Take me to Hala or I take back the sock.

(FAWAZ *pushes* RUND *forward.*)

RUND: Do you always push kids around?

FAWAZ: If they need it.

RUND: I'm not sure I like you.

FAWAZ: Ditto. Now do as I say.

(RUND *shakes* FAWAZ *off her arm and leads the way.*)

(*End Scene Two*)

Scene Three

(HALA *and* MARYAM *are arguing.* HALA *stands on a small stool in her wedding dress.*)

MARYAM: *Hala, Ishlahi elfoustan.* Take it off!

HALA: No. I won't take it off. I'm going to wear it.

MARYAM: Don't be so stubborn!

HALA: I'm going to sleep in it!

(RUND *has lead* FAWAZ *to* HALA.)

MARYAM: Then you will sleep as a fool!

FAWAZ: Hala? Are you Hala?

(HALA *and* MARYAM *are startled by* FAWAZ's *sudden appearance.*)

HALA: Who are you?

RUND: Says he's your brother, Hala.

HALA: What?

FAWAZ: To Be. I'm your brother to be.

(FAWAZ *holds out his hand.* HALA *does not take it.)*

Fawaz Al Haj. Rashid's brother. Older brother.

RUND: *(To* HALA*)* Its true. Too bad, cousin.

(RUND *runs to* HALA *and swishes hard at* HALA's *dress.)*

MARYAM: *(To* FAWAZ*)* Rashid doesn't have a brother.

HALA: *(To* RUND*)* Stop that Rund!

MARYAM: Living. Rashid's brother died.

FAWAZ: What? He said I died? No!

MARYAM: He said you were trampled at a demonstration.

FAWAZ: Trampled at a demonstration? When?

MARYAM: Years ago. Where did Rashid say his brother died, Hala? In D C, I think he said.

FAWAZ: I can't believe it.

MARYAM: The police attacked, the crowd ran and Rashid's brother was crushed under their feet. Tragic. Tragic but courageous.

FAWAZ: I've never been to a demonstration.

HALA: Then you're not Fawaz.

RUND: I want to see your legs, cousin. Are you wearing socks?

(HALA *and* RUND *struggle a moment as* RUND *tries to pull up* HALA's *dress and* HALA *tries to hold it down, uncomfortable in front of* FAWAZ.)

RUND: I need another sock!

FAWAZ: The lying little punk.

HALA: Stop it!

MARYAM: Leave your cousin alone, Rund.

FAWAZ: Why would he say I was dead?

HALA: Stop it, you rascal!

MARYAM: *(To* RUND*)* This is not Hala's day.

(MARYAM *takes* RUND *by the arm and leads her away from* HALA. *They ignore* FAWAZ.)

MARYAM: Rund, my sweet. Go on now.

FAWAZ: Why would he lie?

RUND: No, Auntie!

MARYAM: Get on home!

(RUND *stomps one foot, then runs off.*)

MARYAM: *(To* FAWAZ*)* Whoever you are, you should get home too.

(FAWAZ *gets his passport out and flashes it at* MARYAM. *She glances at the passport, clocks the information and nods to* HALA, *as if to say "Yeah. It's his brother".*)

FAWAZ: Look here, I'm sorry to disappoint you but I'm Rashid's brother. How do you think I knew about the wedding? Because Rashid wrote to me about it. He asked me to come. I didn't want to come. I don't want to be here at all. But my mother begged me because she hasn't seen her son or had a call from him in years. So

I'm here for her, to bring him home. With or without the bride, if that's how it has to be.

MARYAM: The wedding's off.

FAWAZ: What?

MARYAM: Off. Over. Kapute. Kapowed.

HALA: Be quiet, Aunt. *(To* FAWAZ*)* There has been a *(Beat)* postponement.

*(*MARYAM *snorts.)*

FAWAZ: A postponement?

MARYAM: Now take off that dress!

FAWAZ: Where's my brother?

*(*HALA *and* MARYAM *ignore* FAWAZ.*)*

FAWAZ: Hey, where is Rashid? We need to talk.

*(*HALA *stares at* FAWAZ *a moment. Then decides to tell him.)*

HALA: We don't know.

*(*MARYAM *chortles.)*

HALA: We don't know and we don't need to know. He'll be back. No problem. More importantly, why did your brother deny you all these years? What did you do to him?

FAWAZ: I tried to save him from himself. He didn't like that. More importantly, why did he lie to you about me? Not a good way to start a marriage, lying about family.

*(*HALA *looks away.)*

FAWAZ: Cuts both ways, doesn't it? So where is he?

HALA: Go away. I said we don't know.

FAWAZ: I don't believe you. My brother was a liar. Makes sense he'd marry one.

HALA: You are nothing like Rashid. Now leave us. Maryam, there's a button loose. Can you fix it?

MARYAM: Why should I fix it? The wedding is off.

HALA: Today. I'm not getting married today. But tomorrow Rashid will be back and then I'll need this dress. Please. Fix it.

MARYAM: *Affirming:* when I find the needle.

FAWAZ: You're the bride and you don't know where he is?

(MARYAM finds a needle and begins to sew on the button.)

MARYAM: Call in the U N. They're always ineffective.

FAWAZ: Oh. I get it. I get it.

MARYAM: You can hail them like a cab. They drive like cabbies, too.

FAWAZ: Rashid did a runner on you.

MARYAM: *Reaffirming:* you are not getting married.

FAWAZ: I knew it. I knew it!

HALA: Ya Allah. Leave us alone.

FAWAZ: He used to do this to me all the time.

HALA: Do what all the time?

FAWAZ: Mess. Things. Up.

HALA: You don't know Rashid.

FAWAZ: Oh yeah I do. And he's a selfish, thoughtless, disappearing little bastard. *(Sees something on* HALA*'s dress.)* You've got a spot on your dress. Listen, if you and Rashid had problems, maybe I can help. I can tie things up, take you both back home with me. My brother can work in my store.

(HALA bursts our laughing.)

HALA: Rashid work in your store?

FAWAZ: I can get you a green card.

(HALA *finds the spot on her dress.*)

HALA: Mister. I'm not interested in your green card. I have a degree in engineering from the Imperial College of London. I intend to use it here. (*To* MARYAM) Have you got something for a spot?

FAWAZ: I do. Where I come from, travel can be a dirty affair.

(FAWAZ *takes out a spot-remover tissue pack. Hala opens and smells it.*)

HALA: Is this what you sell in your store?

FAWAZ: Yep. Environmentally friendly. Use it on cotton, rayon, and—what happened between you and my brother?

HALA: Keep your nose where it belongs, Fawaz, and not in my business.

RASHID: Well, its obvious you had a bust up.

HALA: (*To herself*) Brother? Huh. My enemy, my brother..

(HALA *starts to clean the spot on her dress but* MARYAM *stops her.*)

MARYAM: Wait! Article 1: Welcoming the solution—I hereby state my concerns about the integrity—of the fabric. It's silk. While Endorsing the British with credibility—disregarding everything they ever promised historically, of course, —I cannot agree. Use salt. Sometimes plain old world peasantries are more effective. Old wives tale, two hundred thirty-two. (*She rummages in her pockets for salt.*)

FAWAZ: That dress is…a good fit.

HALA: It's not for your eyes.

FAWAZ: Rashid's a lucky man.

HALA: Luckiest man in Bethlehem.

(MARYAM *finds the salt and rubs it on the spot as she speaks.*)

MARYAM: Article 2. Concerning the dress: I never liked it. It's too tight.
Article 3. Do you know what your problem is? A. You can't even walk in this dress. B. It's not paid for, and C. Your groom has adiosed because D. He lacks disciplinary imperative.
Article 4. Start over, Hala. But you can't have new ideas while wearing an old fashioned dress.

(MARYAM *now gets out scissors and begins cutting* HALA's *dress until it is manageable, an ordinary garment.* HALA *gasps in shock, but keeps silent.* FAWAZ *watches in fascination.*)

MARYAM: Article 5. Confirming: you were always uncertain about him. That's a fact.
Article 6. Reaffirming: what spins your bolts is gravity and hydraulics.
Article 7. So forget the loser who didn't show, and stick with aerodynamics!
See, you feel better already!

(HALA *looks somewhat dejected, but when she jumps off the stool she looks lighter, fashionable. She spins in a circle, momentarily joyful.*)

HALA: Rashid's going to love this dress!

FAWAZ: Whoa…

(HALA *throws* FAWAZ *an angry look.*)

FAWAZ: As we say back home.

MARYAM: *(To* HALA*)* Article 8. If it's true that Fawaz is his brother, then may Allah help Rashid because that man is not family I would choose. *(She starts to leave but then turns back and looks intently at* FAWAZ.*)* When I reread the Universal Declaration of Human Rights the document came through as the UN-DECLARATION. Then I understood absolutely everything.

(MARYAM *exits.* HALA *gathers up the cut pieces of her dress.*)

FAWAZ: What's up with your Aunt?

HALA: She has a U N stick up her ass. She worked for them for twenty years.

(HALA *puts the dress pieces in Fawaz's arms.*)

HALA: The weather was clear this morning.

FAWAZ: Okay. The weather was clear. But he's an idiot, my brother. To leave you with half a dress.

HALA: Yes. Rashid's an idiot. But a smart one.

FAWAZ: He sure turned your head.

(HALA *studies* FAWAZ's *face.*)

HALA: Your brother is more handsome than you.

FAWAZ: That's not what most cheerleaders thought back in high school.

HALA: Were you always jealous of him?

FAWAZ: *(Laughs)* Is that what he told you? That I was jealous?

HALA: No. But I guessed it.

FAWAZ: He couldn't put two and two together unless I helped him.

HALA: You haven't seen him in years.

FAWAZ: Seven years. I keep count. I missed an important convention to come here: my first invitation to speak at the Association of Family Owned American Health Food Stores. Fully paid. Weekend at the Holiday Inn. The little shit.

HALA: *(Without sentiment)* He says he loved you when you were kids.

FAWAZ: Yeah, well the real issue is: does he love you? And if he does, why did he leave you standing?

(HALA stares hard at FAWAZ. He throws the scraps of dress at her feet then exits.)

(End Scene Three)

Scene Four

(FAWAZ, tired, has been walking with his suitcase. RUND appears.)

FAWAZ: So the weddings off. Hell. What am I supposed to do now? How am I supposed to find Rashid?

RUND: *(Shrugs)* Travel? Yep. You got to travel to find him. Look how easy it is. *(She takes a handful of the map pieces from her pocket.)* It's all here. I can take a handful, see? And travel that fast. Just seconds or minutes. Otherwise, it's hours to get there. And some times not at all. Sometimes never again. But the best way to get around quick, quick is like this:

FAWAZ: Where'd you learn your English?

RUND: Map eating. *(She takes a small piece and eats it.)* Alkhadar. Mint. Yum. Try Beit Jala.

(RUND holds out a piece to FAWAZ. He steps back. She looks through the pieces, looking for a tasty morsel. Finds a piece.)

RUND: Ah. Shit. Here it is again. I ate it yesterday, but each time I eat it, it reappears: Washington, DC. A very Palestinian village. You try. Eat it.

FAWAZ: Stop it, Kid. Things are tough all over. Wipe your eyes. Buck up.

RUND: Buck up. I like that.

FAWAZ: If you know where my brother's run off to, tell me.

RUND: Buck up.

FAWAZ: You're wasting my time.

(RUND *holds out the paper again.*)

RUND: Eat it. Eat it or I will never tell.

FAWAZ: Alright. Give me Washington.

(RUND *holds out the piece to him.* FAWAZ *eats it.*)

FAWAZ: There. Done. Where's my brother?

(RUND *does one of the 21 shoot-to-kill movements she's learned from watching the Israeli Army. But she's modified it to be her own. It's strange and grotesque.* FAWAZ *watches some moments, then grabs her roughly by her collar.*)

FAWAZ: If you've got news for me, give it now and give it fast.

RUND: Wow. Say that again. But meaner this time.

FAWAZ: Tell me what you know right now or I'll, I swear I'll—

RUND: *(Says it for him)* Ram my fist down your scrawny, pitiful throat! Okay, okay, cowboy. I heard. And it's only what I heard. But I heard… And what I heard may not be what I hear tomorrow. I heard…

FAWAZ: Damn it, just spit it out.

RUND: that your brother is involved…

FAWAZ: Yeah?

RUND: If Washington is back again tomorrow I'll consider myself cheated by you.

FAWAZ: Agreed.

RUND: Rashid Al-Haj is involved in an *(Whispers)* operation.

FAWAZ: No. No way.

RUND: I have been eating maps since I was five. My shit is made of paper.

FAWAZ: That's ridiculous. I don't believe you.

RUND: Come after dinner. Usually I poop at that time. I'll show you.

FAWAZ: No. My brother may be a fuck up but he's not a criminal. And he doesn't have the brains to put together any kind of operation. Your info is crap, kid, so don't spread it.

RUND: Look. You need to find your brother. I need to find my school.

FAWAZ: Where's your school?

RUND: It was just about *(Looks around her)* here. But now its gone. The Wall came through and round and snatched it. Now it's on the other side. But I know a crack we could squeeze through.

FAWAZ: I'm not doing anything illegal.

RUND: But you won't get through the checkpoint. They'll stop you.

FAWAZ: Not me, kid.

RUND: Oh yes they will.

Song of the Necessary Permit

RUND: Before you face the M16
From Hebron to Bethlehem,
To pass all checkpoints in between
You gotta have a permit.

From Bethlehem to the city of Ramallah
If that is where you want to go,
You need to say a prayer to Allah
And get a permit.

If you want to pass through the wall,
Go to the hospital or swim the sea,
If you want to die, and be buried at all!
You gotta have a permit.

FAWAZ: They didn't stop me coming in.

RUND: It's a one-way system. You can come in but
usually you can't get out. But we could break your
hand and say you need a doctor.

FAWAZ: This works?

RUND: Sometimes. Probably not. But there's a man at
Sawahreh who has a crane. For a hundred dollars, he
can lift you up, up thirty feet and you can step right
onto the wall. A diving board!

FAWAZ: How do you get off the wall on the other side?

RUND: *(Shrugs)* Never tried it. Give me your other sock
and I'll get you where you want to go.

FAWAZ: You know, your kind give Arabs a bad name.
Ever since I landed all I hear is you people whine.
Can't get here. Can't get there. Can't work here. Can't
work there. And Bethlehem? There's trash everywhere.
Don't you have pick up?

(RUND *just stares at* FAWAZ *until he takes off his other sock
and gives it to her. She takes off her small sock and puts on
the big one. Then she throws her little one at* FAWAZ *who
catches it. He holds it up, gingerly. She looks at her two
matching socks.*)

RUND: Now I'm fully dressed and ready for class. But
where's my school?

FAWAZ: No idea, kid.

RUND: Let's go. If we find my school, we might find
your brother. Your brother always liked school. He had
a pile of books by his bedside that touched the ceiling.
And his favorite was Hemingway.

FAWAZ: Yep. The Old Man and the Sea. But he always fucked things up for me.

(RUND *walks away, then looks back to see if* FAWAZ *is following.*)

(*End Scene Four*)

Scene Five

(*Somewhere in between.* RASHID *sits playing checkers with himself. Each time he moves a checker, he speaks a line. If he makes a mistake in his calculations, he moves the checker back to its place. He is wearing a light harness with ties/ ropes that drag on the ground.*)

RASHID: It was five thirty five in the morning. I slipped in through the window. Hala was asleep. I kissed her cheek. Once. No. Twice. I kissed her on the left cheek twice. She didn't wake. I went down to the basement. We'd built it together. Sort of. Really, she built it but I would do the first test. (*Beat*) The weather was clear that morning so it was all sky. Slick, raw. Seventeen minutes and I landed. No. I didn't land. Yes. Yes. I landed. A good land. A fucking good land. And then. And then. I can't remember. Was it with the takeoff? Think. Think. What went wrong? Retrace. Restart. Was it a problem with the glider's landing? Typical landing approach.

(*Split scene: In another time place,* HALA *is teaching* RASHID, *speaking partly in Arabic, partly in English.*)

HALA: Long steps. Long steps. Resist the temptation to push out the control bar. (*She takes the steps herself, demonstrating.*) Let the wing get its own best trim, best glide. Look for the lift, Rashid!

(*Now* RASHID *hears his name. He leaves his checkers game.*)

RASHID: Baby, how much lean?

(HALA *and* RASHID *are now back in the past. She demonstrates with her body. He mirrors her instructions with his body, arms outstretched like a flyer.)*

HALA: That depends on the wind. But don't shift your feet, just lean forward. Now lean again.

RASHID: *(Leaning)* How much lean. This much?

(HALA *laughs at his awkward "lean".)*

HALA: Habibi, you idiot, no way you're taking my glider on a virgin flight!

(RASHID *shifts. He's doing better.)*

RASHID: This much?

HALA: Better. *(Leaning, showing him)* Now, further.

RASHID: This? Come on, Hala. Let me fly it.

HALA: A little more.

RASHID: You can't build a glider and never fly it.

HALA: Concentrate.

RASHID: If I prove to you that this thing can fly, will you marry me?

HALA: I don't know. Shit, I don't know.

RASHID: Why won't you say yes?

HALA: Now push against the head wind.

RASHID: Well I'm gonna fly the damn thing without your permission and I'll bring you back a gift. Something rare, something wild, as you are.

HALA: Shut up, sweet mouth.

RASHID: I know you want me.

HALA: Lets try take off. *(Beat)* Push the bar. *(She demonstrates.)*

RASHID: Say you want me.

HALA: Push harder.

RASHID: I can smell you, Hala.

HALA: Don't.

RASHID: Touch me, Hala. I'm stiff as a rock.

HALA: Pay attention. Push.

RASHID: I want you.

HALA: Harder, damn you!

RASHID: Please.

HALA/RASHID: Stop. *(They quit pushing.)*

HALA: This isn't an amusement.

RASHID: Neither is love.

HALA: This is not about love. This is about instruction. You could fall out of the sky— *(She snaps her fingers.)* — just like that. Your bones for kindling.

RASHID: I won't ask you to quit teaching or to leave the University. I just want, at the end of each day, to lie down beside you for the rest of my life.

(HALA starts to laugh, but then checks herself.)

HALA: Damn it, Rashid. I can fuse the engine of a motorcycle to a vacuum cleaner.

RASHID: Yeah, and make a vehicle that sucks hard tarmac as it burns down the road.

HALA: If the glider's not in perfect working order. If I make a mistake. If I make a miscalculation…

RASHID: Not afraid to die, Hala. I'm afraid to live without you.

HALA: Stop it. *(Beat)* But I'll make you a deal: you practice to fly it right, practice to fly it like a professional and I'll…

RASHID: Marry you.

HALA: Yes. *(Beat)* But don't ever fly it without me.

RASHID: Done.

HALA: I want a tight dress for the wedding.

RASHID: So tight you can't breathe.

(HALA *smiles, but wonders about this. Then* RASHID *disappears. Only when he's gone does* HALA *suddenly turn as though someone were there, watching her.*)

(*End Scene Five*)

Scene Six

(*At the Bethlehem checkpoint.* FAWAZ *is angrily kicking his suitcase across the stage, back and forth.* RUND *appears and watches him awhile.*)

RUND: Give me that suitcase. You don't deserve it.

FAWAZ: What? No! I already gave you my socks. (*He continues to kick the suitcase.*)

RUND: I lost my book bag. I need your suitcase for my books.

FAWAZ: There's not much in it. Change of shorts. Toothbrush. I wasn't planning a long trip.

(RUND *holds out her hand for the suitcase but* FAWAZ *ignores her and continues to kick it, more like a game now, coming closer to her, and shooting it past her, just missing her.*)

FAWAZ: Those bastards still wouldn't let me pass through.

RUND: Told you so.

FAWAZ: How am I supposed to find Rashid if I can't travel?

(FAWAZ *kicks the suitcase past* RUND's *feet but she stops it, impressively, with her foot.*)

RUND: Practice. And be a soldier. Be a soldier at my checkpoint.

FAWAZ: I don't do games, little girl.

RUND: Kick-the-Suitcase isn't a game?

FAWAZ: No. It's a physical manifestation of Fuck-Travel-In-This-Country.

RUND: Do you miss Rashid?

FAWAZ: No.

RUND: He says he missed you. After you died.

FAWAZ: The liar. I was a damn good brother to him in Cincy. I laid the road and led him by the hand. He never had to worry about a thing. He never even had to think cause I did that for him. I schemed for both of us. And it came to nothing.

RUND: Please. Be a soldier.

(FAWAZ shakes his head "no".)

RUND: If you play my game I'll take you to the man who built the wall: Danny T. The man who invented the wall. They say he knows your brother.

FAWAZ: Bullshit.

RUND: That's what they say.

FAWAZ: They?

RUND: I swear.

(FAWAZ considers, then plays the soldier, barking, with relish.)

FAWAZ: Identification card. Identification card. Identifica—

RUND: Hello soldier. Here's my I D for one school girl, Rund Barghouti, two shoes, two big socks, a ruler, skirt, blouse, *(Whispers)* underpants, *(Loud)* geography book, gum,

FAWAZ: Gun? Gun? She's got a gun!

RUND: No. Gum. Gum. As in chew, chew. But saving it. Tucked away behind my left molar, see?

*(Shows the soldier/*FAWAZ *her left molar.)*

FAWAZ: I could make you spit it out, you know?

RUND: It's double mint.

FAWAZ: Oh. All right then.

RUND: Three hair barrettes.

FAWAZ: I only see two.

RUND: Third one is in my bag in case of emergency.

FAWAZ: There is always emergency. Have some respect.

RUND: And three pencils… And this is when the pencils burst the bag and bust out. It's a jail break! It's astonishing. I hear a rumbling, then a tearing. The soldier hears it too.

FAWAZ: What the hell is that rumbling and tearing?

RUND: I don't hear anything. *(She makes impressive sounds of rumbling and tearing.)* But the soldier will not be fooled!

FAWAZ: I won't be fooled!

RUND: And he calls his buddies.

FAWAZ: Buddies! Buddies!

RUND: And he's rude too!

FAWAZ: Get your asses over here, quick!

RUND: Oh my.

FAWAZ: Two, maybe three pencils. They skedaddled—

RUND: Imagine it. He actually uses the word 'skedaddled'!

FAWAZ: They skedaddled when she opened her bag. But they can't have gone far. Search everyone. Send the women home.

RUND: And tell the men to strip!

FAWAZ: Tell the men to strip! Those pencils, they wouldn't run if they didn't have something to hide.

RUND: "They wouldn't run if they didn't have something to hide." A cliché. We learned that last week in English. And then the soldier says:

FAWAZ: And you, little girlie, plop down right here. You're not going anywhere until we find those pencils and disable them.

RUND: And we know what disabling a pencil means. *(She plops down on his suitcase.)* So I sit down. Three hours later I'm still here. Extra late for school. And that's the whole truth.

(FAWAZ speaks as himself again.)

FAWAZ: So kid, where's this builder who knows about my brother?

RUND: You're a pretty good soldier, Fawaz.

FAWAZ: Thanks.

(RUND picks up his suitcase and begins to leave. RUND motions with her head for him to follow.)

RUND: But next time use another word. A checkpoint soldier would never say "skedaddled".

(End Scene Six)

Scene Seven

(RASHID *is moving along the Wall, as though reading it with his body, arms outstretched.*)

RASHID: *(Sings part in Arablic, part in English)*
Sticky summers, itchy and slow.
and the glides that didn't end.
Why did I leave Cincinnati, oh
My straight roads and the river bend.

(MURAD, *an elderly Jewish immigrant to Israel, and an archeologist, enters pushing a single wheeled measuring contraption ahead of him. He seems to be looking for something in the ground and at first does not "see"* RASHID.)

RASHID: *(Sings)* I took a jumbo jet across the world
And when it landed here, oh yes,
Lemon trees and a pile of shit,
and always garbage burning.
On top of it all, on this mountain of grit,
was Hala, and I was yearning.

(MURAD *runs into* RASHID *with his wheeled contraption, and suddenly "sees" him.*)

MURAD: *Ben zuna!*

RASHID: *Shalom.*

MURAD: Next time announce yourself. You could get shot popping up like that.

RASHID: Shit. *Wein Ana?* What side of the wall am I on?

MURAD: My side. Our side.

RASHID: Which side?

MURAD: Jewish side.

(RASHID *studies* MURAD's *contraption.*)

RASHID: What've you got there?

(MURAD *wheels away.*)

MURAD: I'm an archeologist. Though I'm self-employed. I'm looking for our origins.

RASHID: "Our" origins?

MURAD: The accumulation of time in order to profit. If I find the right site, I'll get a job teaching at Hebrew Unversity! Though Hebrew University doesn't want a man. Like me.

RASHID: Yep. No matter what you find. Hey, can I use that?

MURAD: Certainly not! (*He begins to push his contraption again.*) The measurements must be off.

RASHID: No. You're in the right spot. There are thousands of years of trash on top. It's just deeper than you think.

MURAD: What is "it"?

RASHID: Can I borrow your hammer? (*He lifts the hammer from* MURAD's *belt.*) "It" is the beginnings.

MURAD: The First Temple?

RASHID: Before that. (*He kneels and begins to gently tap the ground.*)

MURAD: There is no before that.

RASHID: Before David and the Israelites: Us. Canaanites.

MURAD: Oh, them. We conquered them.

RASHID: There! There! You hear that?

(MURAD *falls to his knees next to* RASHID *and begins to listen.*)

MURAD: There's definitely a hollow down there. What do you think?

RASHID: It's a tunnel that runs this way. (*He indicates the route.*) You could dig here. Under the wall.

MURAD: Alright. But if the site's late Bronze Age or Canaanite, well then we'll—

RASHID: Bulldoze it?

MURAD: The university will only accept the beginnings. Nothing before that. Everything else…we'll dig it up and throw it out.

RASHID: If you destroy it, the whole thing will collapse. Like a house of cards.

MURAD: The Dividic Empire, the United Monarchy, Solomon's Temple. That is where it all begins. The rest is prehistory.

(*Now* RASHID *manages to snatch the measuring contraption from* MURAD. *He begins to circle* MURAD *while he speaks.*)

RASHID: I've been there. There is no such thing as prehistory.

MURAD: The University says otherwise. This is my calling.

RASHID: So a person can really find something with this, huh? You think it might work for me?

MURAD: Most definitely not.

RASHID: Where you from, old man?

MURAD: My wet nurse was a Muslim. Breast-fed me alongside her own son. I called her Ummi bi'l-riddaa. Mother by nursing.

(RASHID *stops circling now and studies* MURAD.)

MURAD: Baghdad. The oldest Jewish community in the Arab and Islamic world. There were one hundred thousand of us in Iraq.

(RASHID *runs the contraption into* MURAD'*s feet.*)

RASHID: Do you know what happened to me? What did I do that morning? I can't remember.

MURAD: Alright. That's enough now. I order you to leave.

RASHID: But I did something. What did I do?

MURAD: You are corrupting my site!

RASHID: What the fuck happened to me?

MURAD: Silence! *(Beat)* That's none of my concern. I am an archaeologist.

(End Scene Seven)

Scene Eight

(RUND has led FAWAZ to the wall. DANNY T is walking backwards, measuring by his steps.)

DANNY T: It's not a matter of location or geography.

FAWAZ: *(To RUND)* Where are we?

RUND: Shhhhh.

DANNY T: It's a matter of heels and toes.

(RUND disappears.)

DANNY T: Heels and toes.

FAWAZ: Wait!

DANNY T: Seven, eight, nine. Here. Also a bit of there. And "there" is actually more important than "here" because "there" is always in dispute. "There" is out of sight but all we need is. Thirteen, fourteen, fifteen *(He does some fast footwork steps and bumps into FAWAZ.)* A little fancy footwork and there and there, and in any event way over there becomes an indisputable here. Where I'm standing. Mine. And you. You shouldn't be

standing here or there at all. One phone call and you
are "poof". Into air.

FAWAZ: I was told you'd be able to help me: I'm
looking for my brother—

DANNY T: *(Cuts him off)* Oh aren't we all. Aren't we
all? Because it's lonely out here, charting the route,
away from the drills and the dozers. I call them my
bulldogs, the dozers. They get nasty now and then,
and sometimes throw a fit, but they mean well. Scratch
them behind their treads and they're yours for life.

*(For the first time, FAWAZ takes in the enormity and the
height of the wall. DANNY T watches him some moments.)*

DANNY T: What do you think of my dream?

FAWAZ: *(Astonished)* Wow. Fucking hell.

DANNY T: Exactly. A few hundred kilometers at
present. When she's finished, eight hundred and thirty-
two kilometers of hard, hot, can-go-all-night wire and
concrete.

FAWAZ: Impressive, yeah. Of course there are those
who say it's—

DANNY T: Don't say it. Don't say it. "Illegal"? I'm a
architect. I am outside the law. Like flowers and flying
creatures. Do you know why? Because I, Colonel
Danny Tirza, say so. And don't talk to me about the
green line. It's not on our map. We call the line the
Seam Zone and this seam zone is very flexible while
laws are not. As to the health of your people, the wall
will encourage every man, woman, and child to walk
three, four, five times as far, all to the same exit point.
Imagine the exercise! The increased strength in the calf
muscles. The decrease in heart attacks. The lowering
of blood pressure. My friend, what you are looking
at right now is a work of monumental proportions,
an impossible sculpture, a statement etched upon the

land. *(Beat)* I enjoy a bit of poetical language, don't
you?

(Sings)

Song Of The Dream Of Zion

DANNY T:
Oh, ho, what an incredible, wonderful dream:
to re-begin thousands of years of history,
to restart our ancestor's great work, that's the thing,
it's enough to turn the driest eye all teary.

Bathsheba, Bathsheba
Like the land, like the dream,
she's everything, everything.

Oh, ho what an incredible, wonderful dream:
the miraculous rebirth, the light unto nations,
a land without a people, a people with nothing:
has there ever been, sir, such vital recreations?

Bathsheba, Bathsheba,
you just go have her!

It's biblical, archaeological, and really its…right;
you'd be absurd or worse to oppose such a feat,
and like King David and Uriah the Hittite
we'd have to engineer your unhappy defeat.

Bathsheba, Bathsheba
Like the land, like the dream.
You just go have her!

FAWAZ: Mister Tirza. If you've got no info, then let me
pass through this wall.

DANNY T: But Mister?

FAWAZ: Fawaz Al Haj.

(DANNY T registers FAWAZ's name.)

DANNY T: You can't pass through a wall.

FAWAZ: We can be reasonable. We do that in Ohio.

DANNY T: Ohio, huh? I've got an uncle there. Is it all it's cracked up to be?

FAWAZ: At the movie theaters, you can get an extra extra large popcorn. You can get a popcorn so large that you can strap it into the seat right next you and climb inside it, if you don't mind the butter on your shirt.

DANNY T: How entertaining!

(FAWAZ *looks at the wall again.*)

FAWAZ: You really think a people can thrive, trapped behind walls?

DANNY T: Such violent language you people use. Such negativity. "Trapped." They won't be "trapped". They will be cradled within the monument. Have you given a thought to the fact that they'll have wind protection within these walls?

FAWAZ: Hey, it's pretty obvious that you're swallowing the land, uprooting the olive tr—

DANNY T: Oh please. Not the olive-tree-snivel. You people of the olives. The olive tree people. Every time you open your mouth it's about those pits. Talk about oranges for a change. Try some originality.

FAWAZ: History's not always original.

DANNY T: History is a donkey. Beat it with a stick and it will pull the load. (*He begins his "walk" again, back to work.*) As does the Holocaust: an evil so far reaching there's not a piece of history forged on this earth since that hasn't been, in some way, corrupted by this evil. Add to this an appalling history of anti-Semitism endured and our wound was forged. And this wound has, over time, become the scar. My allegiance is to this scar, not its original wound. Because that wound, that very Jewish wound, would not always cooperate. Was not properly ruthless. And truth be told had too much prattle about socialism, brotherhood and anti-zionism for my taste. I am a servant of expansion and consolidation. A servant of pre-emption. In short, I am a servant of the scar.

FAWAZ: Look, Mister Tirza, my apologies. But I don't give a damn about your scar or your wall. I need to find Rashid and get on home.

(DANNY T regards FAWAZ a moment in silence.)

DANNY T: I see. *(Beat)* Well, I believe he just up and left the country.

FAWAZ: Which country would that be?

FAWAZ: Palestine?   DANNY T: Israel!

(DANNY T and FAWAZ are silent a moment. DANNY T goes back to work.)

DANNY T: As a matter of fact, I think he did more than just up and leave. I've heard it said that he "skedaddled".

(End Scene Eight)

Scene Nine

(It is night. Streets of Bethlehem. There is curfew. RUND, carrying the suitcase, springs out in front of MARYAM, who is walking briskly.)

RUND: Give me ten shekels, Auntie! I need to buy a notebook.

MARYAM: *Inti majnounah ya binit!* We're under curfew, Rund. The I D F are looking for someone. Get off the street!

(RUND blocks MARYAM's way.)

RUND: Who are they looking for? What has he done?

MARYAM: There's been an *(Whispers)* operation.

RUND: So they say.

MARYAM: So they say.

RUND: Did they find him? The one who did the operation?

MARYAM: Not yet. So they say.

RUND: So they say.

MARYAM: Now get, little girl.

RUND: Oh it's terrible to be a woman alone. So many choices! Hijab. No hijab. Good thing you're not pregnant. You could go BANG!

MARYAM: I mean it: get home.

RUND: First, play my game: give me five shekels.

MARYAM: You don't have time for games. By the time you try on your first bra the world might be over.

RUND: You shouldn't scare little children.

MARYAM: We don't have time for children. Grow up.

RUND: You're threatening me with apocalypse and Armageddon.

MARYAM: I'm threatening you with restrictive undergarments. Now get out of my way.

RUND: No.

MARYAM: You could be shot.

RUND: Yep.

MARYAM: You could vanish. Pop. Into air.

RUND: Liar.

MARYAM: No. It's true. And you must learn to hold two truths at once, child, and learn that it is crucial to document X in order to declare Y, therefore— reaffirming that each declaration should follow its necessary precedent—

(RUND *puts her hand over* MARYAM's *mouth to shut her up.*)

RUND: Did you ever lose your school?

(RUND *takes her hand away.* MARYAM *speaks more calmly now.*)

MARYAM: Yes. When I was young, I quit the university. Couldn't get to my exams because of the checkpoints and curfews. So I went to work for the U N.

RUND: Did they fire you?

MARYAM: No. But when I tried to get young people like you out of jail, they wouldn't help. They sent some flour instead. With meal worms. So finally I quit. But I still believe in articles.

RUND: Of clothing?

MARYAM: No, child. In articles of law. And one day I'm going to make those articles believe in us. (*Sharp*) But that's enough. Now get off the streets. Or you will disappear too!

(MARYAM *stomps her foot.* RUND *turns to run off then turns back.*)

RUND: But who are they looking for, Auntie?

MARYAM: I don't know.

RUND: Is someone dead? Is someone killed?

MARYAM: I don't know.

RUND: Is someone missing?

MARYAM: Someone is always missing. Now go!

(*End Scene Nine*)

Scene Ten

(HALA *is untangling a roll of wire, rewinding some of it, cutting other bits off, making something mechanical with wire.* FAWAZ *is watching her work.*)

FAWAZ: I'm going in circles, Hala. Two checkpoints and I'm out of Bethlehem, but three more and I still can't get past the Wall. Another two and I'm back here with you.

HALA: Rashid always says "My brother was ace".

FAWAZ: *Is* Ace. "My brother *is* ace."

HALA: Are you Ace, Fawaz? Or just another pack of cards?

FAWAZ: I don't know where to go. No one will tell me anything.

HALA: We don't trust you.

FAWAZ: What are you doing?

HALA: I'm making a model. I need to figure out what went wrong. But it's all such a mess.

FAWAZ: What do you mean "what went wrong"?

HALA: Please. You're distracting me.

FAWAZ: Here, I can help you with that.

(FAWAZ *begins to untangle the wire, but as he does so, he binds* HALA'*s hands, so quickly that she caught off guard.*)

HALA: Let me go.

FAWAZ: Not until I get some answers.

HALA: Who do you think you are?

(FAWAZ *tightens the wire around her hands and arms.*)

FAWAZ: I'm the good guy, okay? I said no to everything I wanted so that kid would turn out right. And what did he do for me in return? He just. Walked away.

(HALA *just looks at* FAWAZ.)

HALA: You've longed for your brother all these years.

FAWAZ: Nope. But my mother has. She's sick with longing. My father died from it.

HALA: Rashid is all you think about.

FAWAZ: I don't give a shit about him. I just need to take him home.

HALA: Maybe you can't find him because you don't know him anymore.

FAWAZ: I know my brother. Time doesn't change that.

HALA: What's his favorite color?

FAWAZ: Blue.

HALA: He mostly wears black. His coffee?

FAWAZ: Milk and lots of sugar.

HALA: No sugar. Doesn't like sweet.

HALA: Favorite season?

FAWAZ: Spring.

HALA: Autumn. Likes the leaves. Favorite pet?

FAWAZ: Dog.

HALA: Canary. What does he sing in the shower?

FAWAZ: I have no idea.

HALA: Neither do I, Ace. Why don't you speak Arabic?

FAWAZ: Because I don't need it.

HALA: You're brother is fluent. He taught himself.

FAWAZ: If you know him so well then where is he? Just tell me and I'll leave you alone.

(HALA *holds out her bound hands for* FAWAZ *to untie her. After a moment, he does, slowly unwinding the wire, getting too close for her comfort.*)

FAWAZ: Well?

HALA: I don't know.

FAWAZ: You don't know? Sure. Right.

HALA: It's the truth.

FAWAZ: Excuse me, Hala, but fuck this place. *(He throws down the wire and starts to exit.)*

HALA: Fawaz Al Haj. There is a lack of respect in your communications with your people.

FAWAZ: Don't start that "your people" stuff with me. My Mother was always after me. My father was, too.

HALA: May he rest in peace.

FAWAZ: I wasn't born here.

HALA: But your father was. That's what Rashid says. *(With emphasis)* Mustafa Al Haj.

FAWAZ: Well, at least Rashid didn't deny their existence.

HALA: Your grandfather was born in the village of Beit Natif, the district of Hebron, in 1929. In 1948, his village was—

FAWAZ/HALA: —attacked by the Zionists and destroyed.

FAWAZ: I know this blather by heart, Hala.

HALA: For two months, your family slept in the fields, waiting to return but every time they did, the soldiers shot at them and forced them back.

(Says the following over and over as HALA *speaks:)*

FAWAZ: La di da. Blah blah blah.

HALA: Your family went to the refugee camp in Bethlehem.

FAWAZ: La di da.

HALA: Your grandfather sold—

FAWAZ/HALA: —tomatoes

FAWAZ: Blah, blah, blah.

HALA: But your father could never accept being—

FAWAZ/HALA: —a refugee.

HALA: That's why he took your mother to the—

FAWAZ: States. Right. My brother-the-idiot—

HALA: —returned and became a West Banker. Why not you?

FAWAZ: Because I'm a resident of the state of Ohio.

HALA: You're a Palestinian, Fawaz.

FAWAZ: Christ. (Mocks) "You're a Palestinian, Fawaz." What does that mean? That I've put my life on hold since 1948? Haven't changed my shoes in fifty years cause the dirt from my village still clings to them? "You're a Palestinian, Fawaz." Yeah. Right. Waiting for the day the sun rises on my ass and sets me alight? My father did that. He died a homesick, nostalgic, frightened old man, and not in his hometown of Beit Natif that he never stopped dreaming about. Know how he died? Buying Graham crackers in the fourteenth aisle of a Kroger shopping mart. Heart attack.

HALA: (Matter of fact) I'd like to visit your zoo in Cincinnati. They say its one of the best in the world. We had a zoo in Rafah. The Israeli Army bulldozed it.

FAWAZ: Look. I quit crying over spilt milk when I got old enough to wipe my chin. Why don't you try it?

(FAWAZ and HALA just stare at one another.)

FAWAZ: Or better yet, take off that scarf.

HALA: No.

FAWAZ: Let me see your hair.

HALA: Never.

FAWAZ: You know its no big deal where I come from. Its just hair.

(HALA just looks at FAWAZ.)

HALA: Why don't you take something off?

FAWAZ: I'm not wearing a scarf.

HALA: Your shirt, then. Go on. Take it off.

(FAWAZ glances about him, uncertain.)

FAWAZ: You sure? *(Beat)* Would you like that, Hala?

(FAWAZ starts to unbutton his shirt. HALA smiles. He undoes another button. Then she slaps him in the face.)

HALA: Button your shirt, Yankee. When an abandoned bride asks the brother of her beloved to take off his clothes he's supposed to take pity on her. He's supposed to say "no". Say it, "No".

FAWAZ: No.

HALA: Thank you. *(Beat)* Now go find Rashid. Bring him back to me. And then leave us alone.

(End Scene Ten)

Scene Eleven

(MURAD and RASHID at night, in a garden in the Israeli settlement of Gilo. MURAD sits on a chair. As he speaks, RASHID is looking for a particular piece of ground)

MURAD: *(To himself)* Miss Baghdad had a mole on the side of her neck. No. Somewhere strange. In her armpit. In the shape of a fish. *(Sees RASHID)* Oh. It's you again. Sit down. Would you like a cup of tea?

RASHID: No thanks.

MURAD: Do you have friends? I am looking for friends. But what are you doing on this side of the fence again?

RASHID: Wall.

MURAD: *(Shrugs)* Whatever.

RASHID: Where am I?

MURAD: The Gilo settlement. You're meshtahim, from the West Bank. A West Banker!

RASHID: I'm lost.

MURAD: So am I. Though I know where I am. *(Beat)* You're breaking the law just to stand here.

(RASHID seems to have found what he's looking for.)

RASHID: Buddy, it's been a long day. You've no idea. Now get up.

MURAD: How did you pass through the barrier? Hmm. You're not the first, you know. This morning, I saw another one like you. He was in the air. Flying. A flying man. I said "Good morning, Flying Man." And he said— *(He calls as though from high up:)* "Good morning, brother." He called me brother. Even when I live on this side. I appreciate that. I said "What's your name?" But he was disappearing into the sky by then. I think he said..

RASHID: Rashid.

MURAD: Yes. Rashid. Would you like a biscuit?

RASHID: Move your chair. Just to there.

MURAD: Why?

RASHID: That's mine. Was. My Mom and Pops grew up here. Under your chair. Long ago. I never was able to make it over here before. Just want to step on it a few times. For old times sake.

MURAD: Please. Don't be sentimental. Me, I've always lived on both sides of the coin: lucky and unlucky, hero

and traitor, dreamer and destroyer. Yet I do believe in
fairy tales. Why else would I stay here? We dreamed
of a bi-national state, Jew and Arab living side by side.
It was possible. See? Both sides of the coin. But here
is the rub: I labor against any messianic bullshit and
end up living in a messianic nation. Do you think Miss
Baghdad could have loved a skinny runt of a peasant's
son?

RASHID: I doubt it.

MURAD: Get out of here. You give me the shivers!

RASHID: Just let me look at that piece under your chair.
I just want to look, old man. Please. Just move.

(MURAD *finally gets up and moves the chair.* MURAD *and*
RASHID *look at the spot of earth.* RASHID *steps on the spot
triumphantly.*)

MURAD: Hey.

RASHID: Now I'm home again.

MURAD: Excuse me?

RASHID: Home on the range. Right on this spot.

MURAD: Move, please. I must put my chair back.

RASHID: This was our palace, old man. This is it. And I
need to feel the dirt on my soles.

MURAD: This is unacceptable.

RASHID: You're damn right it is.

(RASHID *begins to take off his shoes.* MURAD *watches him.*
RASHID *enjoys his bare feet on the ground while* MURAD
speaks.)

MURAD: This is your palace, hmm? Mine was in
Baghdad. We wanted to stay in Iraq. It was our home.
But we would be saved even though many of us did
not want to be saved. The politicians made secret deals
to evacuate the entire community of Baghdadi Jews by

air and bring us here. But they didn't talk to us. The French and British were the bastards, really. They did all they could to widen the gap between Arab and Jew. A bitter wind. But a wind that began in Europe, not in Iraq.

(RASHID *lets out a howl of glee, ignoring* MURAD, *happy to be "home".*)

MURAD: Don't laugh at me. I listen to Farid al-Atrache.

RASHID: And Umm Kalthum?

MURAD: Yes. And Mohammed Abdel Wahab. But at a checkpoint, I could shoot you dead. Then go home to my family at night.

RASHID: You know, there comes a time when a guy needs to take a serious road trip.

MURAD: I am lonely. I need a friend.

RASHID: Lift off, leap frog over the obstacles,

MURAD: My name is Murad Salih Daniel. I am an Arab Jew.

RASHID: glide out of the turbulence, and dig in deep. Take a stand.

MURAD: I cannot go back because this is now my country. But I'm still a stranger here after so many years.

RASHID: Damn, its good to be back in the 'hood.

MURAD: I am a nigger in the land of the Jews.

(*End Scene Eleven*)

Scene Twelve

(FAWAZ, *this time from the other side of the stage, is thrown/shoved through the air and lands hard, sprawling. He is disheveled and rants with all the energy he's got left. The quotes are I D F soldiers speaking, which he imitates/ mocks.*)

FAWAZ: That's the last time you shove me, buddy! I'm an American citizen. You hear me? You don't shove Americans! You don't search Americans! "Why are you here?" I don't want to fucking be here! If I could I'd flush this noxious, putrid, dirty, crumbling beast of a country—countries!—down the compactor. Yeah! Yeah! "We are looking for someone." Well I hope you never find him. I don't know you people. I don't care about you people. "But you're not only an American, are you?" (*He lets out a long howl of rage.*) Mister Asshole. I have to find my brother. Then I'll get out and I'll never come back. "His name? His name?" I won't tell you. I won't tell you his fucking name. (*Calls out*) Where are you? You little shit. You double-crossing, back-stabbing, piece of…Palestinian shit! Ha. Yeah. Ha. You eat that one, Rashid!

(RASHID *enters, from the past, carrying* FAWAZ's *suitcase, as though it were his own. He sets it down between them. After a moment* FAWAZ *is also back in the past.*)

RASHID: These are the facts: I love the air.

FAWAZ: No, you're obsessed with it.

RASHID: Yep. 'Cause its better up there than down here. So I'm flying across the ocean, bro. I'm going home to Bethlehem.

FAWAZ: Yeah. Mom told me. I told her not to worry cause I won't let you.

RASHID: I'm eighteen now.

FAWAZ: You're going to join me at University next fall. Everything is on track.

RASHID: Fawaz. I'm already packed.

FAWAZ: Then I'll help you unpack.

RASHID: You want to drive me to the bus station?

FAWAZ: Rashid. Don't you dare.

RASHID: We're Palestinians.

FAWAZ: We're Americans.

RASHID: We're Arab-Americans. That in itself is un-American.

FAWAZ: Stop it. You're hurting them. Mother's walking at night. Father just stares.

RASHID: They're just afraid.

FAWAZ: Of course they're afraid. They think you'll never come back.

RASHID: I'll just go and check things out. Find the place where mom and dad grew up. I won't stay.

FAWAZ: You're not going anywhere. I won't let you ruin our plans.

RASHID: But there's not enough space for me here. I'm falling even when I walk.

FAWAZ: It's called being a teenager. Get over it.

RASHID: I'm going.

FAWAZ: You won't have any rights over there. None. Only as a tourist. You think it will feel like home?

(RASHID *doesn't answer.*)

FAWAZ: Answer me. You think Bethlehem will feel like home? You've never been there. How could it feel like home? Answer me.

(RASHID *won't answer.*)

FAWAZ: Answer the goddamn question, Rashid. Will it feel like home? *(Beat)* No. It won't. Not ever. This is your home. Right here, with me.

RASHID: *(Changing tactics, relishing)* Brother. They say the women there make a sound when you touch them. A kind of hum and it makes you so hard you weep. I'm going to find me one of those women. *(He makes a humming sound.)*

FAWAZ: Stop it.

RASHID: Why don't you come with me?

(FAWAZ laughs in exasperation.)

RASHID: Don't make me go alone.

FAWAZ: If you leave, I won't come after you.

RASHID: We could go together—

FAWAZ: *(Interrupts)* Don't start.

RASHID: I don't want a steady job. I don't want to pay my taxes, put up an above-ground swimming pool in my back yard. I don't want a bar-b-que—

FAWAZ: What the fuck is wrong with a bar-b-que?

RASHID: I just want to find some..

FAWAZ: Fucking common sense?

RASHID: Yeah. Something like that. So when I wake up in the morning and step out of bed, it matters. When I walk outside, it matters. When I speak to another person, it matters—

FAWAZ: *(Interrupts)* Hold it right there, bud. I'm gonna call the talk shows right now 'cause thats the kind of cold, hard, intelligent thinking that everyone needs to hear. *(Beat)* Nothing you can do over there is going to make a difference because without me, you're too small, Rashid. Without me, you're just a fucking kid.

RASHID: I'm your brother.

(FAWAZ *suddenly turns on* RASHID, *furious and afraid.*)

FAWAZ: Then don't leave me!

RASHID: I have to.

(RASHID *tries to get past* FAWAZ *to leave but* FAWAZ *blocks him.* RASHID *tries again and* FAWAZ *blocks him. Then* FAWAZ *loses control and knocks* RASHID *down and pummels him, hard.* RASHID *doesn't fight back. As* FAWAZ *repeatedly hits and kicks* RASHID, *he shouts the following:*)

FAWAZ: You're not going anywhere! You're not going anywhere! You're not going anywhere!

(FAWAZ *suddenly quits beating* RASHID *and gets off him.* RASHID *lies still a moment, stunned and battered. Then he painfully, slowly, gets up, picks up the suitcase and leaves. Only after* RASHID *is gone does* FAWAZ *call to him. His call echoes all around him.*)

FAWAZ: Rashid! Wait. Come back!

(*The* CHORUS *appear as* SOLDIERS, *having heard* RASHID's *name.*)

FAWAZ: *(Calling)* You come back here, you bastard! Don't leave us alone. Rashid! Rashid Al-Haj! Come back.

(FAWAZ, *collapsed in grief, doesn't see the* SOLDIERS. *Now, the* SOLDIERS *dance and their dance is both muscular and graceful. The song begins as heartfelt but becomes increasingly ironic.*)

Song Of The Yearning Youths

SOLDIERS: When we were little tots,
we licked our lolly pops.
When we hit puberty
we hankered for our liberty.

Then the black letter came.
We had to leave our game.

We put down the soccer ball.
We left our shoes in the hall.

(Refrain) We missed the kiss in the dark.
We missed the girl in the park.

Slippers for army boots.
Sling shot for a gun that shoots.
Snug bed for the all night watch.
Sweet dreams for the lonely crotch.

We say we are not afraid
that soon we will meet our grave.
Mother, can you bring me home?
Daddy, don't leave me alone.

(Now, the SOLDIERS *circle* FAWAZ, *who is crouched on the ground.)*

SOLDIERS: We missed the kiss in the dark.
We missed the girl in the park.

(The SOLDIERS *perform, one at a time, six shoot-to-kill positions. These positions are accurate and frightening.* FAWAZ *slowly "wakes" into their reality and raises his arms, frozen.* RASHID *appears, and from another world, he watches.)*

SOLDIERS: Fawaz Al Haj.
Fawaz Al Haj.
Fawaz Al Haj.
Brother to the Terrorist Rashid Al Haj.
Brother to Terrorist Rashid Al Haj.
We got you. We got you. We got you.

(FAWAZ is arrested and handcuffed. Suddenly RASHID *understands.)*

RASHID: So that's what happened. *(Beat)* I'm dead.

(FAWAZ hears RASHID'S *voice and at the same moment the brothers lock eyes.)*

(There is the loud bang and the echo of a cell door closing. Many cell doors closing. Blackout.)

(End Scene Twelve)

END ACT ONE

ACT TWO

Scene One

(RUND *enters with the suitcase, opens it, and takes out a handful of flower bulbs. She stands on the suitcase as though it were a box. She juggles the bulbs as she chants.*)

RUND:
Wild flowers. Wild flowers. Where are my friends?
I hear them on the playground, but I can't see them.
Wild flowers. Wild flowers. Can you hear that quick
    bell?
Time to study for geography, new maths or old hell.

(DANNY T *appears. He snatches the bulbs from* RUND.)

DANNY T: Where did you get these?

RUND: They have an underground storage system, these Geophytes.

DANNY T: Yes. Wild flowers. Begin. Begin! (*He now acts as her teacher.*)

RUND: The organ, the bulb, allows them to survive through difficult times of heat and dryness. As the Wall is built, Israel will move eight thousand-five hundred bulbs to a temporary home until it is time to replant them safely.

DANNY T: Quite right. With the help of Israflora, we will invest one-point- two-five million shekels in locating, marking, digging up, and replanting thousands of rare bulbs. Stand up straight when you speak to the class.

RUND: You have counted each orchid and tulip.

DANNY T: And?

(RUND *can't remember.*)

DANNY T: Chin up. Shoulders back. Enunciate clearly. And?

RUND: Iris. Each orchid, tulip and iris.

DANNY T: The rarer blooms are marked individually.

RUND: Bulbs in larger groups are marked as clusters.

DANNY T: It would've been cheaper to buy a few thousand new bulbs from a nursery and plant them but?

RUND: But we are strict—

DANNY T: Wrong pronoun. Eyes straight ahead. Wide, wide. Surprised almost. As though you had spotted, well, myself in your classroom!

RUND: But *you* are

DANNY T: Yes.

RUND: But you are strict about returning the original flowers to their natural habitat. You are so strict you will be returning the original soil to replant the bulbs.

DANNY T: Yes, we will be returning the original soil to replant the bulbs. Correct. Correct. This way, no foreign genetic material is introduced. Five stars for the girl on the box.

RUND: You're not my teacher. Where is Fawaz?

DANNY T: Exactly where he should be.

RUND: What have you done to him? Where is my school?

DANNY T: Ah, now there are some things even Danny T cannot answer.

(RUND *jumps off the suitcase.*)

RUND: Give it back! Give me back my school!

DANNY T: Perhaps your school didn't like you and just up and left.

RUND: No. Wrong answer. Get on the box. Get on the box!

(DANNY T *gets on the suitcase.*)

RUND: Ears back. Eyes straight. Leg in the air!

(DANNY T *attempts to follow* RUND's *instructions.*)

RUND: Now. Who are you?

DANNY T: I'm your new classmate.

RUND: No. Arms out. Hair up. Who are you?

DANNY T: I am…I am…an architect who drew such lines on history that it didn't have a chance to mark me.

RUND: I am a bulb.

DANNY T: A bulb?

RUND: Yes. I am a bulb.

DANNY T: You are a girl.

RUND: No. I have an underground storage system that allows me to survive under difficult circumstances.

(DANNY T *quits his posing.*)

DANNY T: Kid, you are confusing yourself with a geophyte.

RUND: Wrong. Sit at the back of the class.

DANNY T: Geophytes live in the ground.

RUND: No star for you! Now write one hundred times: You are a bulb.

DANNY T: No.

RUND: And you relocated me.

DANNY T: Actually, we plucked you out. We needed the room.

RUND: Say it: *you are a bulb.* Say it or my storage system will explode.

DANNY T: My, my. All right. You are a bulb.

RUND: Yes. I am a bulb. And I will return to my original soil.

(RUND *disappears.* DANNY T *examines the bulb, thinking.*)

(*End Scene One*)

Scene Two

(FAWAZ *is in jail in Jerusalem. Three soldiers from the* CHORUS *are interrogating a shape on the ground, as large as a man, but it's not a man. The* CHORUS *slowly circle the shape, making distorted movements with their bodies.* FAWAZ *watches them, mesmerized. The brutality should be suggested, stylized, and force used only where indicated in the script.*)

SOLDIER 1: That was a kiss. Just a little kiss. (*Beat*) You want another one? Another smaker-oo?

FAWAZ: Hey. What are you doing?

SOLDIER 2: Oh, oh, oh. Are you crying, sweetheart?

FAWAZ: Stop it! Leave that man alone!

SOLDIER 3: Let me see those tears.

(SOLDIER 1 *kicks the shape on the ground.*)

FAWAZ: Shit. Look at his face. You kicked him in the face.

SOLDIER 2: We have a paper for you to sign. Are you willing to sign? Mister Al Haj?

(FAWAZ *realizes the shape being beaten is himself. He moves in closer to have a look.*)

FAWAZ: Fuck. That's me.

SOLDIER 3: Just sign the paper to admit you were involved with your brother's Operation. And we'll be nice to you.

SOLDIER 1: No? No? Okay. Then I'm going to kick your ass and every time you have to count.

SOLDIER 2: When the number is high enough, let me know and he'll stop.

SOLDIER 1: (*Gives the shape a kick*) Count. (*Another kick*) Count you motherfucker or I'll call in my buddies and we'll do it with the band.

(*He goes to crush* FAWAZ'*s head with his boot but* FAWAZ *starts counting, steadily.* SOLDIER 1 *doesn't see* FAWAZ *but he hears the counts*)

FAWAZ: One.

SOLDIER 3: That's right.

(*Kicks him.*)

FAWAZ: Two. I won't sign.

SOLDIER 2: Again.

FAWAZ: Three. What did my brother do?

SOLDIER 1: Four.

FAWAZ: I had nothing to do with it! Five.

(FAWAZ *stops counting and sings the torture song. The* SOLDIERS *continue the interrogation throughout the song, but they move into slow motion, stylized*).

Song: When Torture Is Good For Your Health

FAWAZ:

I've been sleeping all my life, it took you to wake me.
I'll do anything you want, only make sure you make
  me.
Take away all sight and sound til I all I do is weep.
I can feel it growing big, yeah the love is growing deep.

*(Refrain)*Torture makes you heat up, makes your blood
  run clean.
Torture takes you places where you've never even
  been.
Torture makes you flexible, torture makes you real.
Torture teaches you to open, teaches you to feel.

Kick me in the gut again, you can make me dance.
Shock me in the groin and I'll shit in my pants.
Hang me from my wrists and I'll surely be your friend.
Choke me with cold water and I'll love you 'til the end.
I will love you…

(He stops singing and then calls out in despair.) Rashid!

(FAWAZ's voice echo's through the cell, then the prison, as he collapses onto the shape on the ground.)

(End Scene Two)

Scene Three

(MURAD appears and finds RASHID in his garden. RASHID's eyes are closed and he's listening to something. We can still faintly hear FAWAZ call his brother's name. MURAD pushes RASHID but RASHID holds his ground.)

MURAD: I thought I kicked you out? You ingrate.

(RASHID shoves MURAD back. It is as though the shoving were a part of the conversation.)

RASHID: Nah. I bounced back. You trespasser. Weather's been great.

(MURAD *shoves* RASHID *again, harder.* RASHID *holds his ground.*)

MURAD: What is it you want? God's pig.

RASHID: Right now I want…a space. Ass-bone! *(He shoves* MURAD *back, harder.)* A space to piss.

MURAD: How dare you!? You will not piss in my garden!

RASHID: Now that I've settled in, I think I'll put in some tomatoes. Never seen so much water.

MURAD: Ha! Diverted from the West Bank. Operation Oasis. For our settlements. Looks like vacation houses in Switzerland.

RASHID: So I could plant oranges?

MURAD: Oranges.

RASHID: Grapes?

MURAD: Grapes.

RASHID: Lemons?

MURAD: Lemons!

RASHID: My brother's somewhere out there, I can feel it. Know where he is?

MURAD: Only rumors: that he never left his store in Ohio. That he took a detour and he's drunk in the Louvre. That he jumped off the Hilton in Amsterdam.

RASHID: Well. I'm going to bring him to this spot. My father walked here. Ate here. My mother too. Sex even. Maybe right on this spot.

MURAD: No! No! There is no sex on this ground.

RASHID: Their moans are in the grass. Hear them.

(RASHID *makes mournful "masculine" moans.*)

MURAD: Well, if that was the sound your father made, young man, then it doesn't sound like your mother was getting much action.

RASHID: I don't like you.

MURAD: And I don't like you.

(MURAD *and* RASHID *are silent a moment together.*)

MURAD: But this is not about liking.
This is about.

RASHID: Yeah. This is about..

(MURAD *and* RASHID *both sing their lonely song, apart and together.*)

The Wandering Song Club

MURAD:
There's no place in the world for us,
once we've left, we are gone,
there's no one to go back to
we just move on, we move on

I'm from the wandering song club
I'm from the wandering song club

RASHID:
Nowhere is a sand pit
A river full of spit
we are thirsty, we are hungry
we have no place to shit

MURAD/RASHID:
I'm from the wandering song club
I'm from the wandering song club

(RASHID *takes out a dirty old flask.*)

RASHID: I've been saving this. Was my great Uncle's.

MURAD: Yuck. It is rusted. When was the last time he drank from it?

RASHID: 1948. Come.

(RASHID *shares his water, dripping it into* MURAD's *mouth.*)

MURAD: Are you living alone?

(RASHID *casts a glance around his tiny space.*)

RASHID: Not sure. Yeah, maybe. At present. I was going to get married but I died.

MURAD: Yes. I heard that rumor, too. *(Beat)* Is it possible…could it be possible…might you need a roommate? Only to cut expenses, of course. Two is cheaper than one.

(RASHID *does not move.* MURAD *waits. Then* RASHID *slowly and carefully moves just a couple of inches over.* MURAD *comes and squeezes in next to him, into his space.*)

MURAD: Yes. You are right. It's actually quite spacious.

(MURAD *and* RASHID *stand tightly together in the space, side by side, in silence for some moments.*)

MURAD: In Baghdad they used to say that if you lose someone, talk to your feet and they will lead you. The foot is a compass.

RASHID: Yeah? Well there's not a compass in this God forsaken land that isn't broke. But thanks. I'll give it a try. And now I gotta piss. Turn around please.

(MURAD *manages to turn around, staying within their shared space.* RASHID *pisses into* MURAD's *watering can then returns it to* MURAD. *When* MURAD *turns back around,* RASHID *is gone.*)

(*End Scene Three*)

Scene Four

(FAWAZ *is still in jail, collapsed on the floor. He begins to hallucinate.* HALA *enters humming happily. She has a white bridal veil over her face and is completely covered. There is something frightening about this vision.*)

FAWAZ: Who are you?

HALA: Shhh… (*She hums.*)

FAWAZ: I know who you are. You're my brother's woman.

HALA: Your brother has no woman. He's a sweet, dead man. And I'm not really here.

FAWAZ: You are

HALA: (*Secretive*) Yoni.

FAWAZ: Hala.

HALA: Shhh. It's a secret. You're not supposed to know.

FAWAZ: You shouldn't be here.

HALA: You shouldn't be here. This is the women's side.

FAWAZ: I mean I shouldn't be here. Either.

(MARYAM *enters. She ignores* FAWAZ.)

FAWAZ: I can't. Leave.

(MARYAM *takes off* HALA's *veil.*)

HALA: He won't leave.

MARYAM: Never mind. Maybe he'll learn something!

(HALA *and* MARYAM *giggle together.*)

MARYAM: There are limited methods, maneuvers, and mechanics, but there are endless techniques. Let's begin with the twenty one positions of love. Essentially there are five positions, and the other sixteen are built upon them: 1) he is on his back and you are on top, 2) you are on your back and he is on top, 3) you are facing each other, 4) you have your back to him, or 5) you are seated facing each other. What's your pleasure?

HALA: All of the above.

(HALA *rolls up her sleeves to get ready.* HALA *and* MARYAM *are enjoying themselves.*)

MARYAM: One. A goblet shaped six petalled bloom. Two. Double cypress. Three. Curving outward.

(HALA *demonstrates some of the "positions" by herself. She ignores* FAWAZ, *who watches her, fascinated.*)

MARYAM: Four seven blooms per branch. Five sometimes parrot.

HALA: Parrot?

MARYAM: That's what the book says.

HALA: What does that mean?

MARYAM: Squawkers?

HALA: Imitators?

MARYAM: Talkers.

HALA: Oh, I like the talkers.

MARYAM: Really? I like quiet. A little breath. That's all.

HALA: No, I like when he says:

(*From a good distance.* HALA *whispers, in Arabic, the things she likes to hear.*)

FAWAZ: No.

HALA: No? Yes.

(*Now,* HALA *repeats the postures. This time* FAWAZ *is "moved" by them, his movements mirroring hers. He is being tortured by these involuntary positions his body is making.* HALA *never touches him.* FAWAZ *is in an extreme pain that wants to be pleasure.*)

FAWAZ: No. Stop it. You're burning him.

MARYAM: Eyes,

FAWAZ: Me.

HALA: nose,

MARYAM: ears, fingers,

FAWAZ: Stop.

MARYAM: throat.

FAWAZ: Please.

HALA: I love when he says please.

FAWAZ: Me.

MARYAM: The mouth.

HALA: You've told me nothing about the mouth.
(Moving so close she could kiss him.)

FAWAZ: *(Coming to)* No. No. I can't. Please.

(HALA and MARYAM begin to perform the positions together as the CHORUS enters and joins the women in these more aggressive, yet still beautiful, positions.)

MARYAM: There are limited methods, maneuvers, and weapons, but there are endless techniques.

FAWAZ: You don't belong here.

MARYAM: There are limited methods, maneuvers, and blood but there are endless techniques.

FAWAZ: I don't belong here.

SOLDIERS 1/2/3: There are endless techniques.

(SOLDIERS all surround FAWAZ and take him in their arms.)

FAWAZ: Damn you. Give me back my fingernail.

(Then FAWAZ is suddenly alone again. He passes out.)

(End Scene Four)

Scene Five

(FAWAZ is still asleep in his cell. RASHID is standing over him.)

RASHID: Hey big brother. You're looking kinda small since I saw you last?

(RASHID nudges FAWAZ with his foot. FAWAZ startles "awake".)

FAWAZ: Shit, Rashid. You're dead.

RASHID: Haven't seen him in years. First thing he says "Shit, Rashid. You're dead." You sure know how to do reunion, don't you? Did you see my Hala? Not a woman so fine. Ice and water. Vinegar and salt. She's a mechanical engineer. Knows where things fit.

FAWAZ: What did you do?

RASHID: I went for a ride in Hala's flying machine.

FAWAZ: You killed someone.

RASHID: No.

FAWAZ: Yes you fucking did or I wouldn't be in here taking your beating.

RASHID: Maybe you threw a stone?

FAWAZ: Where am I?

RASHID: An Israeli jail, called Mascubiya A K A the Russian Compound. In West Jerusalem. I didn't kill anyone.

FAWAZ: But you tried.

RASHID: I did what needed to be done. I took action, brother.

FAWAZ: You sound like a fanatic.

RASHID: Don't sign. They'll release you in a few days. How bad are you hurting?

FAWAZ: I didn't know the human body could withstand that kind of impact.

RASHID: I love Hala. I want you to know that.

FAWAZ: Then why did you fuck things up?

RASHID: Did you miss me?

FAWAZ: We didn't hear from you for years so we got used to it. Why'd you tell people I was dead?

RASHID: *(Shrugs)* The last time I saw you, you hit me twenty seven times.

FAWAZ: You deserved twenty eight.

RASHID: That's why. That's exactly why, Fawaz. You haven't changed.

FAWAZ: Fucking neither have you.

(RASHID laughs.)

RASHID: Ah, but I fell in love. I was so happy that last morning. The years that lay ahead of me and all made up of her. Of Hala. She laughed when she was sad. It was like a bell in my chest. You know what was the best part? I could turn my head to the left or to the right and see her standing there, like a miracle, right beside me.

FAWAZ: You don't deserve her. *(Beat)* She's beautiful.

RASHID: If Hala will have you, you can have her. I mean that.

FAWAZ: But she's yours.

RASHID: Not anymore. I won't say I'm happy about it but rather you than anyone else.

FAWAZ: Hala doesn't like me.

RASHID: Hala wouldn't look you in the eye when she met you. That means she likes you. And you better appreciate that. Hala doesn't like a lot of people. *(Beat)*

Fawaz. I need you to find out how I died. And why. I can't rest. I can't even be dead like I'm supposed to be. I need a picture in my mind.

FAWAZ: You're dead. Aren't you all knowing?

RASHID: Now that's the kind of crap you Breathers make up. Look, not knowing what I did, not knowing what happened to me because of it, I've never felt that kind of pain.

FAWAZ: I'm in jail. I can't do anything. But soon as I get out of here I'm going back. Home.

RASHID: Home. Always liked that word. Kind of like a horn. Home. (*Says the word "hooooooome" like a horn.*) Home.

FAWAZ: You know this will finish Mom off, don't you? (*Beat*) Why did you leave us?

RASHID: I never could sleep when we were kids. This country kept me awake. First time I ever slept right was the night I landed here. Without sleep we die. I didn't want to die.

FAWAZ: Yeah, well father died.

RASHID: I know.

FAWAZ: But you couldn't bother to come home, not even for his funeral. Mom stopped speaking. Even to me. So I did it alone. I did it all alone. Everything. You fuckin' sand nigger. Rag head.

RASHID: Injun Joe. Salami Sam.

FAWAZ: Camel fucker!

RASHID: Yeah. Those were the good old days at Ranger Grade School. Sometimes I miss those endearments.

FAWAZ: It's not so bad once you get older.

RASHID: Sure. (*He spits on* FAWAZ.) How about that one? I bet you still get that one?

FAWAZ: I'm still alive. You're dead. So who's the smart ass?

RASHID: Ouch. Goal. *(Beat)* I'm sorry about Dad's funeral.

FAWAZ: Easy to say now.

RASHID: If I'd left here they wouldn't have let me back in. I couldn't risk it.

FAWAZ: Fuck you.

RASHID: So what do you think of this country?

FAWAZ: Dirty

RASHID: Poor

FAWAZ: Crowded

RASHID: Pissed off

FAWAZ: Hungry

RASHID: *(Celebrating)* And fully occupied. Yeah! Have we got the edge on paradise or what?!

FAWAZ: You're not better looking than I am.

RASHID: Maybe not. But I'm younger.

FAWAZ: Not anymore.

(FAWAZ and RASHID just eye one another some moments.)

RASHID: This is the center of the earth, Fawaz. What goes down here will go down in Cincinnati, will go down everywhere. You know that.

FAWAZ: Rashid. Don't start.

RASHID: 'Cause we're a people who never quit. We're a people—

FAWAZ: Bullshit. You know what we are, brother? You know what we are? We're a people who fight for a homeland for fifty years and at the pinnacle of negotiations for a state of our own we show up without a map. Without our own fucking map. It's shameful. The corruption of our leaders. Our shabby compromises. Our ignorance of Israel. Our—

RASHID: *(Takes over for him)* cult of personality. Our general lack of seriousness. Our corrosive divisions.

FAWAZ: Exactly. There's no point.

RASHID: We've got to keep working. Readjusting our sight lines.

FAWAZ: Even after sixty fucking years? Just words, Rashid. Just words.

RASHID: Yeah. But choosing the right ones. Keeping the pace against all that diminishes us, diminishes everyone around us. That's what it's about. Being alive, Fawaz. It's about being alive.

FAWAZ: There are other ways to be alive.

RASHID: Yeah. But they kill the libido. Resistance is good for your erections.

FAWAZ: Whatever you've done here is. Meaningless. Nothing has changed and you're dead. So I'll always be. Without you.

(After some moments)

RASHID: Find out what happened.

FAWAZ: I can't.

RASHID: We need you. Here.

FAWAZ: Sure. Maybe I could tear the wall down with my own bare hands, huh?

RASHID: Now doesn't that get you hard just thinking about it? *(Beat)* Promise me you'll stay here.

FAWAZ: *(With finality)* I'm going back to the States.

RASHID: Okay. Okay, sure. Well, say good-bye, Bro.

(FAWAZ just stares at him.)

RASHID: Say good-bye. But answer me one question: does it feel like home? Your sweet Ohio city, does it feel like home? Hey. *(He pushes* FAWAZ.*)* Hey. Answer the question. Does it feel like home? *(He pushes* FAWAZ *harder, until he answers him.)* It's not a difficult question. Answer me, Fawaz. Answer the God damn question? Does Cincinnati feel like home?

FAWAZ: Yes.

RASHID: Still the liar you've always been.

FAWAZ: *(Shouts)* It feels like home.

*(*RASHID *just stares at* FAWAZ. *Then disappears.)*

FAWAZ: Right here, Rashid. With you.

(End Scene Five)

Scene Six

(Jail compound. Three SOLDIERS *as jail clerks, fully loaded. Maryam, disguised in big sunglasses.)*

SOLDIER 3: We don't speak Arabic.

MARYAM: You understand English: I'm here to obtain the release of Fawaz Al Haj.

SOLDIER 1: All we know in English is "hello!"

SOLDIER 1/2/3: Hello!

MARYAM: What are the charges against him?

SOLDIER 2: And "how are you?"

SOLDIER 1: Soldiers—

SOLDIER CHORUS: Yes, please!

MARYAM: Boys. Article 1) whereas disregard and contempt for human rights have resulted in barbarous acts—

SOLDIER 3: English please!

SOLDIER 2: *(To* SOLDIER 3*)* What's barbarous?

SOLDIER 1: You cook on it!

SOLDIER 2: That's a bar-b-que.

MARYAM: Article 2) Whereas he is allergic to dust and, Article 3) peanuts. Therefore he could asphyxiate. Article 4) And furthermore you will be held responsible.

SOLDIER 3: *(To* SOLDIER 2*)* What is "asphyxiate"?

SOLDIER 1: This is a war! Are you kidding?

MARYAM: Article 5) His clean underwear and socks. Article 6) Concerning democracy.

SOLDIER 3: Oh Democracy!

MARYAM: Article 7) "Be a light unto nations."

SOLDIER 2/3: No thank you!

MARYAM: Article 8) Reaffirming their determination to live in peace—

SOLDIER 1/2/3: Aagh! The P word!

MARYAM: Article 9) Recognizing that peace requires the transition—

SOLDIER 1/2/3: Aagh! The P word

SOLDIER 3: You want to take away our jobs?

SOLDIER 2: You think we want to sit on the beach all day?

SOLDIER 3: And look at girls?

SOLDIER 1/2/3: Huh?

MARYAM: Article 10) "Objective: to attack the village of Kibya. 11) occupy it and cause maximal damage 12) to life and property" Major Ariel Sharon.

SOLDIER 2: Why you pickin' on Sharon?

MARYAM: Article 13) Affirming that this agreement marks the recognition of the right of the Palestinian—

SOLDIER 2/3: The P word!

MARYAM: Article 14) the equal rights of respected citizens.

SOLDIER 3: Now just who are you calling citizens?

MARYAM: Fawaz al Haj. He's a disagreeable man.

SOLDIER 1/2/3: Never heard of him.

MARYAM: Arrogant, and stubborn as a mule.

SOLDIER 1/2/3: Never heard of him.

MARYAM: But he's family. Article 15) "All existing things are really one". Chuang Tzu. I thought it might be. Possible.

SOLDIER 1: Lady. One more P word and you're done.

The P Song

SOLDIERS: Let's call someone. You know, we don't want visitors here.
You woke us from our naps, when you leave we'll crack a beer.
No (permits) No (peace) No (possibilities)
Don't' give me that don't give me that
No words that start with P

MARYAM: Article 16) Raise your Black Flags boys: Refuse to obey manifestly illegal orders.

SOLDIER 3: How does she know about the black flag?

SOLIDERS: This is out of hand. We're just here to protect our borders
This is how we do this. Don't be messing with our orders.

No (permits) No (peace) No (possibilities)
Don't give me that don't give me that
No words that start with P

MARYAM: Article 17) Refuse to serve in the territories.
Article 18) whereas this situation is not heavenly
ordained. 19) This is collective punishment.

SOLDIERS: *(Sing)* No permits No peace No possibilities
Don't give me that don't give me that
No words that start with P

MARYAM: Article 20) In the name of all declarations,
release Fawaz El Haj.

SOLDIER 2: That's twenty.

SOLDIER 3: Twenty?

SOLDIER 1: What's twenty one?

MARYAM: That I will never tell you.

SOLDIER 1/2/3: Huh???

MARYAM: I'll stay right here until you get him.

(End Scene Six)

Scene Seven

*(FAWAZ has been released from jail. He is sitting huddled on
the street, bruised, disheveled, dirty, and disorientated. After
some moments RUND appears. She studies FAWAZ. FAWAZ
doesn't respond to her.)*

RUND: I need to buy new pencils. Give me five shekels.
(Beat) Alright. Then give me four.

*(FAWAZ doesn't respond at all, just stares into space. RUND
cocks her head.)*

RUND: They were looking for someone. I guess they
found *you*.

(As FAWAZ *still doesn't respond,* RUND *shrugs, then searches his shirt pocket. She finds one of her socks. She searches another pocket. Finds her lost sock. She holds the two socks up and examines them.)*

RUND: My other sock! I knew it had been arrested. You must have found it in Mascubiya. Thank you, thank you. Now they're together again. *(She looks down at the big socks she's wearing.)* But I've got new socks for school. *(She looks at* FAWAZ's *bare ankles.)* You don't have any socks. You can keep my old ones.

*(*RUND *rests the socks, one each on top of* FAWAZ's *shoes.* FAWAZ *is still in a daze. Then* RUND *kisses* FAWAZ *on the cheek.)*

RUND: Wake up. *(Beat)* Please. Wake up.

(Now FAWAZ *comes out of his daze. He looks at* RUND *and really takes her in. She takes a handful of map pieces from her pocket.)*

RUND: Do you want your map back?

(After a long moment, FAWAZ *holds out his hand.* RUND *lets the pieces of map sprinkle and fall into his hand. Some of the pieces fall onto the floor.* DANNY T *appears at the other end of the stage, carrying* FAWAZ's *suitcase. He and* RUND *eye one another. She runs away.* FAWAZ *ignores* DANNY T. FAWAZ *begins to pick up the tiny map pieces, carefully noting each piece and putting it into his pocket.)*

DANNY T: I heard they let you out. *(Beat)* Thought you'd need this, for your return journey.

*(*DANNY T *shoves the suitcase with his foot and it slides across the stage and comes to rest beside* FAWAZ.)*

DANNY T: Did you know that your Arafat, God rest his soul, named me Abu Kharita? Father of the map.

*(*FAWAZ *continues to pick up the map pieces as he speaks until he's gathered them all into his pocket.)*

FAWAZ: *(Quietly)* What if the people miss the wind?

DANNY T: What?

FAWAZ: What if the people behind your wall miss the wind? No reason to open the windows anymore because there is no breeze. Might get angry. Might get very pissed off. *(He has finished gathering the pieces.)*

DANNY T: Are you threatening me?

FAWAZ: Yes.

DANNY T: Are you going to get extreme?

FAWAZ: Send you a rocket? Or strap on a belt, step on a bus, blow as many Israelis to pieces as possible? Nah.

DANNY T: Don't be too hard on yourself. We kill your civilians as well. At a nineteen to one ratio.

FAWAZ: I think you mean ninety to one.

DANNY T: *(Shrugs)* I am not in denial. But what bothers me is your particular way of killing. We use apaches, missiles. Or bullets. Quite often to the head. But we keep our distance. You, on the other hand, you kill yourselves inside our buses—

(FAWAZ moves to face DANNY T.)

FAWAZ: Inside your cafes, inside your restaurants? We murder you so close up we can smell your fear and you can see ours. We kill ourselves inside you.

DANNY T: That kind of intimacy is unforgivable.

FAWAZ: How did my brother die?

DANNY T: I'm under no obligation to tell you anything.

FAWAZ: He needs to know.

DANNY T: Your brother is dead. Are you feeling alright? Perhaps they went a little hard during questioning?

FAWAZ: I need to know.

DANNY T: *(Holding out the suitcase)* What you need to know is the time your flight leaves. Go home, Fawaz. *(Beat)* Go home.

(FAWAZ slowly takes the suitcase as though to leave but then walks right up to DANNY T until their noses are touching.)

DANNY T: And what the hell is this?

FAWAZ: This. Is. Me. And I think I'm going to stay right here forever.

DANNY T: Even forever gets tired and goes away.

FAWAZ: Not my kind of forever.

(DANNY T and FAWAZ stare each other down some moments.)

FAWAZ: I've only been here a few days and already I can't breathe. The maps have more to do with cloud formations than the facts on the ground. Every day you take a little more. Your wall is the skyline. Today I read that you opened your first butterfly festival. I can hear your laughter on the other side.

DANNY T: You complain about our laughter?

FAWAZ: When you're finished most of the settlers will live outside the wall. Eighty-nine percent of Palestinians will be trapped inside it.

DANNY T: *(Sharply)* This wall is a necessity!

(FAWAZ speaks into DANNY T's ear. He begins his "no" as a whisper, then builds. Then the "no" seems to come from around them, not just FAWAZ's voice.)

FAWAZ: No.

DANNY T: To protect us.

FAWAZ: No.

DANNY T: From your voices.

FAWAZ: No.

DANNY T: From your hunger.

FAWAZ: No.

DANNY T: From your intimacy.

FAWAZ: No.

DANNY T: From your blood lust.

FAWAZ: No.

DANNY T: From your murder.

FAWAZ: Say it once. Just this once: your wall. Your dream. Its about acquisition. It's about real-estate.

(DANNY T turns around.)

DANNY T: *(Explodes)* Yes. Real-estate! *(Calmly)* With papers from God.

(DANNY T and FAWAZ eye one another, neither budging. RASHID appears. FAWAZ and RASHID are aware of one another but DANNY T does not see RASHID nor does RASHID look at DANNY T. DANNY T speaks to FAWAZ, though sometimes he might "hear" RASHID.)

FAWAZ: My brother will haunt you.

(DANNY T considers this.)

DANNY T: I'm going to be up front: I don't believe in ghosts.

RASHID: Let me be equally straightforward: I don't believe in Zionists.

DANNY T: You want to know how he died? That's what they all want to know. Can't you people be a little more alert in your last moments of life?

FAWAZ: What did my brother do?

DANNY T: *(Suddenly angry)* Your brother attempted to disrupt our… Operation.

FAWAZ: What operation?

DANNY T: Operation Geophyte, we call it. The Battle of the Bulbs.

RASHID: I woke at five thirty-five in the morning. Still dark. I slipped in through the window. Hala was asleep.

DANNY T: In actuality, an Operation of compassion: we save the bulbs as we build the wall. Then we replant them.

RASHID: It was our wedding day. I kissed her cheek. Twice. I zipped up my jacket and wanted to shout 'cause I felt so damn good.

DANNY T: Your brother stole one of our bulbs.

FAWAZ: My brother is dead because of a bulb?

RASHID: *(Remembering)* The bulb! Shit…

DANNY T: Not just any bulb. We discovered it two meters west of marker 186: the rare single bee orchid.

FAWAZ: My idiot brother wasted his life to steal a bulb?

DANNY T: Your brother was, in actuality…brilliant. He found a way to hurt us that did not kill us. That kind of strategy, I envy.

FAWAZ: The single bee orchid, huh?

RASHID: Its pretty cool, bro.

DANNY T: To have seen it in bloom. You would have wept.

FAWAZ: Yes. I think I would have.

RASHID: Not some flowers from the corner store but something rare as Hala: the single bee orchid.

(Split scene. HALA and RUND appear. DANNY T, FAWAZ and RASHID do not see them, nor do HALA and RUND see the three men).

FAWAZ: So how did he die?

DANNY T: I'll tell you—

RUND: I'll tell you, Hala.

HALA: *(To* RUND*)* But how could you know that?

DANNY T: —if you promise to leave me in peace.

RUND: I was looking for my school.

FAWAZ/RASHID: Agreed.

RASHID: And then I lifted off.

HALA: In the dark?

RASHID: That's the best time to fly.

RUND: That's when I saw Rashid.

RASHID: Then it was all sky. Slick, raw.

RUND: He went over the wall in the glider.

FAWAZ: Fuck. A glider.

RUND: Yes, a glider.

HALA: Cruising Speed?

RUND: It wasn't his speed.

FAWAZ: He knew how to fly.

RASHID: I did everything right.

DANNY T/RUND: I saw what happened.

RUND: Yes. He flew over the wall without a sound.

FAWAZ: No one could glide like my brother.

HALA: Did he stall in the air?

RUND: There was no stall, Hala.

RASHID: Damn it.

HALA: He didn't have the speed.

RASHID: Seventy kilometers.

FAWAZ: Did he lose his speed?

RUND: Stop it, Hala. It wasn't—

RASHID: My speed.

FAWAZ: He wouldn't make that kind of mistake.

DANNY T: He didn't make a mistake.

HALA: He touched down?

RUND: Yes.

DANNY T: Yes.

RASHID: A precision spot landing,

FAWAZ: full flare.

HALA: Then he got what he came for?

DANNY T: Yes. He got what he came for: the orchid.

RASHID: The orchid. For my bride. I stole for Hala what was already ours.

RUND: Then Rashid re-launched.

RASHID: Full gas with between-the-teeth

FAWAZ/RASHID: clamp type accelerator.

DANNY T: He started running. Long steps. Long steps.

HALA: With a ten kilometer headwind.

FAWAZ: You looked for the lift, Rashid!

RASHID: I got the lift!

HALA: But he didn't get the lift.

FAWAZ: Fuck.

RUND: And then he began to fall.

HALA: The wind wasn't right. He started to fall.

DANNY T: He started to fall.

RASHID: Shit.

DANNY T/RUND: And then our/their soldiers shot him.

(Some moments of silence)

FAWAZ: Well I'll be damned. So Rashid almost made it.

RUND: He almost made it.

RASHID: I almost made it. Hala.

(HALA *hears* RASHID *say her name. They suddenly "see" one another and speak directly to each other. There is a quiet joy in their meeting.)*

RASHID: You told me not to fly the glider, Hala. But I had to—

HALA: —couldn't resist. I know. There were things I could not, could not—

RASHID: —foresee. I needed to show you I could fly it. It's all right. I don't—

HALA: —regret. Only that I was not—

HALA/RASHID: —with you.

HALA: Our plans. Our wedding. Mine—

RASHID: —and yours. It was almost a—

HALA/RASHID: —success.

HALA: I wish we could—

RASHID: —begin—

HALA/RASHID: —again.

HALA: It was, always, my sweetheart,

RASHID: My love, always, it was—

HALA/RASHID: You.

(RUND *takes* HALA's *hand and they leave.* RASHID *watches* HALA *go.)*

FAWAZ: No. *(Beat)* No. No. No. No. No. No. No. No. No. No. No. No. No. No. No. No. No.

(FAWAZ *says "No" over and over, to himself, to* DANNY T, *to* RASHID's *death, to everything around him, saying "No" maybe 30 or 40 times.* DANNY T *and* RASHID *watch him.*

When FAWAZ *is empty of "No"s he quits. Silence for some moments.)*

DANNY T: Fawaz Al Haj. I saw your brother in the air. I saw his glider come over the wall.

RASHID: Then why did you wait? Why didn't you shoot me right then?

(Overlapping)

FAWAZ: Why didn't you shoot him right then?

DANNY T: I'd been up all night with my charts. We were just about to start work to close the last wall section around Bethlehem in area three. I looked up from my office, which is my four by four. I looked up, and there he was: a man in mid-flight, floating down, something from another time. Something poured from the grace of one world into the next. I could not move. So, so. Extraordinary. Audacious. Yes. And I could not speak. I just watched him. And for the first time in so many, many years I wanted something else.

FAWAZ: What did you want?

DANNY T: I wanted to be up there, in that peaceful sky. I wanted to defy gravity. I wanted to be. You.

(For the first time, DANNY T *looks at* RASHID *and sees him. But* RASHID *keeps his eyes on* FAWAZ *and nods his thanks.* FAWAZ *leaves.* RASHID *now looks at* DANNY T *for the first time and they lock eyes. After some moments,* RASHID *exits.* DANNY T *looks around; he is alone again.)*

(End Scene Seven)

Scene Eight

(MURAD *wears a pair of designer sunglasses; he's in a new*
"under cover" outfit. MARYAM *is also wearing sunglasses.*
She studies MURAD's *glasses.*)

MARYAM: Ray ban or Police?

MURAD: Klein. Calvin. Yours?

MARYAM: Russian.

MURAD: They can get you anything, those guys. I was
an archaeologist. But I couldn't get a job. Now I'm
security. Security, security, security.

MARYAM: It's a growth industry. Can I try on your
sunglasses?

MURAD: Sure.

(MARYAM *and* MURAD *exchange sunglasses.*)

MURAD: Not bad. Nice weight to them. Hey. Sky looks
sort of. Black. With these on.

MARYAM: Hmmm. Ground looks kind of bumpy. With
these on. Big bumps. This how you see?

MURAD: Hey. With these you look a foot smaller.

MARYAM: Now you are a good meter taller!

MURAD: I like this. You don't look like much trouble
now. Hey, I'm looking for a little girl. Her name is
Rund. Rund Barghouti.

MARYAM: What do you want with her?

MURAD: If you see her, tell her that security has located
her school and it's still intact. Though not fully. It
seems it was a hundred percent until we halved it.
Then we had to take another twenty-four percent. But
today she can have the rest, which is about twenty-two
percent and includes the toilet and art room. But while
we can't give her a hundred percent of the twenty-two

percent that's left, we can give her fifty-seven percent of the twenty-two percent that's left, which means of the toilet we may still have to take the plumbing and of the art room, we'll need the floor.

MARYAM: So many pieces are missing. How to put the puzzle back together again? (*She begins to leave.*)

MURAD: Hey!

(MURAD *takes off his sunglasses.* MARYAM *and* MURAD *exchange sunglasses.*)

MURAD: It was Humpty Dumpty who needed to be put back together again. After his fall.

MARYAM: Yes, after his fall. From the wall. But when he fell, it wasn't his shell that broke into a thousand pieces. It was the ground beneath him.

(MARYAM *sings and, in places,* MURAD *joins in. Before the song finishes they are both gone but we still hear them singing into the next scene.*)

Maryam's Song

MARYAM: Sleep, sleep my little one
Tomorrow your father comes
With a bag full of lemons

Sleep, sleep, my little one.
Tomorrow your mother comes
with a bundle of sticks.

Sleep, sleep, my little one
You know when you wake,
You'll only keep waiting.
You'll always be waiting.

(*End Scene Eight*)

Scene Nine

(RUND *runs in*)

RUND: I found my school!

(*Now we hear the* CHORUS *counting off-stage.* RUND *listens to the counting then speaks to* DANNY T *and public*).

RUND: I'm sorry I'm late. I ran into some (*Spells quickly*) O-B-S-T-R-U-C-T-I-O-N-S. What? So this is not spelling class. Is it music? Or Dance?
All right.

(RUND *dances a traditional Palestinian dance in time with the* SOLDIER'*s counting. Then the* SOLDIERS *enter. If possible there are suddenly many* SOLDIERS. DANNY T *joins them. They perform their twenty-one shoot-to-kill positions. The count is part of the dance.* RUND *begins to mimic the twenty-one positions back to the soldiers as she sings.*)

RUND: (*Sings*)
If I'm standing in the path of the wall as you
build it, soldier tell me, will it cut me in two?

Will one of my arms and one of my legs sit in class
and do maths and the other arm and leg play in the
　　grass

by the swings? But where will my head go, I'm losing
　　track,
which side of the wall? How will my pieces find their
　　way back?

And how can there be the other side of Bethlehem,
when there is only one, only one Bethlehem?

(RUND *and the* SOLDIERS *stop dancing.*)

RUND: (*To* DANNY T) Wow. I did great. How many is
that?

DANNY T: That's twenty one.

RUND: Twenty one what?

DANNY T: Twenty one shoot-to-kill positions.

RUND: Do I get a star?

(In answer, the SOLDIERS, *now in various shoot-to-kill positions, raise their guns, aiming at* RUND. *She takes a couple of steps backwards but doesn't flinch just stares hard back at them.)*

RUND: I can see. You. Can you. See me?

(Then after some moments, DANNY T *touches each soldier on the shoulder and they lower their guns one by one and exit.* DANNY T *and* RUND *lock eyes. She exits.)*

(End Scene Nine)

Scene Ten

(With a simple tape measure, HALA *is taking measurements of the ground. And the air. She hums a similar tune as* MARYAM *sang. After some moments,* FAWAZ *appears.* HALA *stops measuring and they regard one another.)*

HALA: How tall are you?

FAWAZ: Not as tall as my brother. Was.

HALA: I heard you buckled up. Called ahead for a no-carb meal and flew back across the ocean.

FAWAZ: Hala.

HALA: I'd say you just miss six feet.

FAWAZ: Why did you build the glider?

HALA: Because I could.

FAWAZ: You knew Rashid was crazy about those things.

HALA: Of course. That's why I built it.

FAWAZ: Rashid said as a kid he was always falling. He didn't mean falling as in falling down. It was something inside him that kept giving way. I think while he lived here with you he stopped falling.

HALA: Mister Al Haj, its too late for sentiment. I have objects to measure. Go away.

FAWAZ: You made a mistake, Hala. I'm six feet tall exactly. Go ahead. Measure me. Maybe you got it wrong.

(HALA approaches FAWAZ with the measuring tape and just eyes him. Then she kneels down and measures him, all the way up from his feet to his head, careful not to touch.)

FAWAZ: Bingo.

HALA: I still love Rashid.

FAWAZ: So do I. *(Beat)* How about my shoulders, straight across.

HALA: Thirty-one inches. I will always miss him. *(She measures his shoulders.)*

FAWAZ: So will I.

HALA: Twenty nine and a half.

FAWAZ: Not even close. You're out of practice. My neck, around.

HALA: Fourteen inches. *(She measures.)* Bingo.

FAWAZ: My face.

HALA: Eight. *(She measures.)* Rashid will always be with me.

FAWAZ: My eyes, corner to corner. And with me. I wish I'd known him better.

(HALA measures, slowly, now letting the tape touch FAWAZ's skin, finding his face with the tape measure.)

FAWAZ: My mouth.

HALA: Open or closed?

FAWAZ: *(Uncertain)* However you want it.

(HALA *measures* FAWAZ's *mouth. Then suddenly, almost accidentally, they kiss with the tape measure between their mouths. She breaks the kiss off.*)

FAWAZ: Could we try that again?

HALA: Not now. I'm in mourning. And I have classes to prepare for. Adding to this, I'm building something new in my basement. Don't you have a plane to catch?

FAWAZ: Lost my suitcase. Makes it hard to travel.

HALA: It might not work out, Fawaz.

(FAWAZ *and* HALA *regard one another some moments.*)

FAWAZ: Did you know that to get into my brother's room when we were kids you had to go down on your hands and knees?

HALA: No. (*Beat*) I didn't.

FAWAZ: It was that crowded. I think even he was embarrassed by it.

(RASHID *appears and as he appears a model glider drops down from above and hangs over their heads.*)

FAWAZ: He had forty seven model gliders hanging from his bedroom ceiling. It was crazy. No, it was fucking amazing. And so was he. I was lucky he stayed around as long as he did.

(FAWAZ, HALA, *and* RASHID *are now all looking up.* RASHID *is on his knees, looking up.*)

FAWAZ: You know, Rashid used to say:

RASHID: Fawaz. When I'm up in that glider, there is no plan. And all of its possible. Up in that glider, there's just

FAWAZ/HALA/RASHID: wide open space.

(*Now the stage grows darker as many gliders appear and hang over them.* FAWAZ, HALA *and* RASHID *continue to watch the small gliders that begin to glow in the dark like many tiny lights or stars.* R*und appears, stands close behind* R*ashid, and watches the gliders, too. She makes the buzzing noise of the glider's motors.* R*ashid joins her in this sound. Slowly the room fills with this noise until it is deafening. Then sudden, complete silence, and black out.*)

END OF PLAY

Partial Bibliography/Further Reading

Armstrong, Karen. *Islam: A Short History.* New York: The Modern Library, 2002.

Cohen, Mark and Abraham Udovitch. *Jews Among Arabs.* Princeton: The Darwin Press, 1989.

Chacham, Ronit. *Breaking Ranks: Refusing to Serve in the West Bank and Gaza Strip.* New York: Other Press, 2003.

Hass, Amira. *Drinking the Sea at Gaza.* London: Hamish Hamilton, 1999.

Hass, Amira. *Reporting from Ramallah: An Israeli in an Occupied Land.* Cambridge: M I T Press, 2003.

Khalidi, Rashid. *The Iron Cage: The Story of the Palestinian Struggle for Statehood.* Boston: Beacon Press, 2006.

Kushner, Tony, and Alisa Solomon. *Wrestling with Zion: Progressive Jewish-American Responses to the Israeli-Palestinian Conflict.* New York: Grove Press, 2003.

Makdisi, Saree. *Palestine Inside Out: An Everyday Occupation.* New York: W W Norton & Company, 2010.

Nathan, Susan. *The Other Side of Israel: My Journey Across the Jewish-Arab Divide.* London: HarperCollins, 2006.

Pappe, Ilan. *The Ethnic Cleansing of Palestine.* London: Oneworld Publications, 2007.

Reinhart, Tanya. *Israel/Palestine: How to End the War of 1948*. New York: Seven Stories Press, 2002.

Reporters Without Borders, editors. *Israel/Palestine: The Black Book*. London: Pluto Press, 2003.

Reuter, Christoph. *My Life is a Weapon: A Modern History of Suicide Bombing*. Princeton: Princeton University Press, 2002.

Rose, John. *The Myths of Zion*. London: Pluto Press, 2004.

Said, Edward. *After the Last Sky*. New York: Columbia University Press, 1999.

Said, Edward. *The Question of Palestine*. New York: Vintage Books, 1992.

Shehadeh, Raja. *Palestinian Walks: Forays into a Vanishing Landscape*. New York: Scribner, 2008.

Shehadeh, Raja. *When The Bulbul Stopped Singing: A Diary of Ramallah Under Siege*. London: Profile Books, 2003.

Rodinson, Maxime. *Israel: A Colonial-Settler State?* New York: Monad Press, 1973.

Warschawski, Michel (translated by Levi Laub). *On the Border*. Cambridge, MA: South End Press, 2005.

Weizman, Eyal. *Hollow Land: Israel's Architecture of Occupation*. London: Verso, 2007.